AMETHYST

~ *and* ~

AGATE

D1564255

AMETHYST
~ and ~
AGATE:

Poems of Lake Superior

Edited by
JIM PERLMAN, DEBORAH COOPER,
MARA HART, PAMELA MITTLEFEHLDT

HOLY COW! PRESS
DULUTH, MINNESOTA
2015

Permissions and additional copyright notices appear on pages
153-157; copyrights for the individual poems in this collection
are held by their authors.

Cover art, "Lake Superior," watercolor on vellum (1991) by
Nancy Hemstad Seaton.

Grateful acknowledgement to Penny Perry for her selection
and arrangement of Lake Superior visual art that is included
in this collection.

Book and cover design by Anton Khodakovsky.
Printed and bound in the United States of America.
First printing, 2015
ISBN 978-0-9864480-1-0
9 8 7 6 5 4 3 2 1

This project is supported in part by grant awards from the
Ben and Jeanne Overman Charitable Trust, the Elmer L. and
Eleanor J. Andersen Foundation, the Cy and Paula DeCosse
Fund of The Minneapolis Foundation, the Lenfestey Family
Foundation, and by gifts from individual donors.

Holy Cow! Press books are distributed to the trade by
Consortium Book Sales & Distribution, c/o Perseus
Distribution, 210 American Drive, Jackson, TN 38301.

For inquiries, please write to:
Holy Cow! Press, Post Office Box 3170, Mount Royal Station,
Duluth, MN 55803. Visit www.holycowpress.org

TABLE OF CONTENTS

xiii   Amethyst and Agate: An Introduction

1   Gichigami
Dan Campion

3   Solstice
Angela Ahlgren

4   At the Koitto Boarding House, 1947
Angela Ahlgren

7   Oligotrophic
James Armstrong

9   Windbound with Dostoevsky
Milton J. Bates

11   Counterpoint
Samuel Black

12   Slippage
Kimberly Blaeser

14   Eloquence of Earth
Kimberly Blaeser

16   After Sailing
Gary Boelhower

18   Dance at Dawn
Gary Boelhower

19   The North (After Borges)
Jeffrey D. Boldt

20   Angling for Whitefish
Taina Maki Chahal

23   The Ice is Coming in like an Animal to the Shore
Sharon Chmielarz

25   Sailing in the Moon's Wake
David R. Clowers

26   After Matthew Arnold's "Dover Beach"
David R. Clowers

27   In Dreams
Carolyn Colburn

28   Across the Border
Deborah Cooper

31   After All of My Life
Florence Chard Dacey

32   Superior at the Shoreline: February
Norita Dittberner-Jax

33   Levitating Toward Duluth
Norita Dittberner-Jax

35   Water Colors
Deborah H. Doolittle

36   Wishing for Lake Superior
Deborah H. Doolittle

38   Freighters Slide By
Barbara Draper

40   Gitche Onigaming, Grand Portage
Heid E. Erdrich

42   Manidoo Giizhikens: Little Spirit Cedar Tree
Heid E. Erdrich

45   Wooded Road, Lake Superior
      Michelle Bonczek Evory

47   Lake Superior Spring
      Teresa Boyle Falsani

48   The Work of Water
      Teresa Boyle Falsani

50   Crossing the Continental Divide
      Lynda Ferguson

52   Voyageur
      Phil Fitzpatrick

54   Lake Drought
      Margot Fortunato Galt

56   Northwestern Ontario
      Julie Gard

"Breakwater 1" *by AJ Atwater*; "North Dakota Kayaks" *by Sue Pavlatos*; "View from Oberg Mountain" *by Alberta Marana*; "Superior Dawn" *by Cecilia Lieder*; "Temporal Display" *by Penny Perry*; "Untitled (Flow)" *by Sarah M. Brokke*; "Hidden Anchorage" *by Thomas Rauschenfels*; "At the Shore" *by Cecilia Lieder*

57   Watermark
      Jane Graham George

59   Crossing Over
      Candace Ginsberg

60   The Great Lake
      Linda Glaser

62   Night Sky
Tom Hansen

63   Messages
Gwen Hart

65   After Forty-Three Years
Mara Kirk Hart

66   Gooseberry Falls, Duluth, Minnesota
Susan Carol Hauser

68   Lake Superior
Susan Hawkinson

70   I Tell the Lake a Story
Eva Hooker

73   There is work to do within nothingness
Eva Hooker

75   Into All Things We Enter
Ann Iverson

76   Speaking to Lake Superior Elders
Janet Jerve

78   Hawk Ridge
Jim Johnson

81   Agates
Meridel Kahl

82   To Begin Again
Meridel Kahl

83   In Concert, the Fluency
Maggie Kazel

85   Spirit Little Cedar
Susan Deborah King

87   Late Ice
     Mary F. Lee

88   Easter Dawn on Superior
     Cecilia Lieder

89   Shovel Point
     Judy Lindberg

92   Key Sequences Missing
     Micky McGilligan

93   Lake Superior Poem
     Lisa McKhann

96   Poet Laureate of Duluth
     Pamela Mittlefehldt

99   Sailing Superior
     Yvonne Pearson

100 Temperance 2020
     Susan Perala-Dewey

     "Brighton Beach" *by Arna Rennan*; "Full Circle" *by
     Adam Swanson*; "Across the Border" *by Joel Cooper*;
     "Reflected Sea" *by Thomas Rauschenfels*; "Apostle
     Island Shore" *by Jan Wise*; "Sky and Life" *by Adam
     Swanson*; "Sea Creatures" *by Thomas Rauschenfels*

101 Stockton Island
     Kenneth Pobo

102 Apostle Fall
     Kenneth Pobo

103 The Big Sing
     Mary Riley

105   Yooper Rockhounds
Mary Riley

106   Lake Superior Poem #3
George Roberts

107   Welder
Mary Kay Rummel

109   Fishing
Yvonne Rutford

110   Morning
Ellie Schoenfeld

112   An Unrefined Northern Metaphor
Ellie Schoenfeld

114   Mining Country
Steven Sher

116   Some Distance Offshore
Phillip Sterling

118   Lake Superior Beachcombing
Amy Jo Swing

121   Lake Superior—A Love Song from the Lake
Sara Thomsen

123   A Random Gust from the North
Connie Wanek

129   Cartography
Laurelyn Whitt

132   métis
Laurelyn Whitt

135   Making the Lake My North
Morgan Grayce Willow

137   Night Swim in Lake Superior
Patricia Zontelli

139 Notes on Contributors

153 Permissions and Sources

159 About the Cover Artist

161 About the Lake Superior Artists

163 About the Editors

Amethyst and Agate:
An Introduction

"Who knows the lull and longing?
This ancient scented language
is sand, shells, and spray
the call of sea gulls and mystery. . ."
Kimberly Blaeser, "Slippage"

GICHIGAMI. SWEET WATER SEA. Shining Big-Sea Water. Lake Superior. It is scavenging gull and mystery. Agate and driftwood. Sea smoke, memory, desire. It sings to us "in syllables/of sapphire/and silver," as Meridel Kahl writes. In its ancient language we hear legend and story. It thunders. It is mute. Jane Graham George observes that the "mind imprints what it loves." Lake Superior has been imprinted on mind and memory, in dreams and poems.

We, the four editors of *Amethyst and Agate*, had completed two anthologies, *Beloved on the Earth: 150 Poems of Grief and Gratitude* and *The Heart of All That Is: Reflections on Home*, and were in search of a focus for a new anthology—one that would speak about place, that would honor our connection with this earth. We were moved by the Mother Earth Water Walkers and the Grandmothers on the *Nibi*/Water Walks, honoring the Anishinaabe belief that water is life and that the People are the keepers of the water.

We wondered how poets listen and speak to water—particularly the waters of Lake Superior. How are poets keepers of this water? We put out a call for poems about Lake Superior. The poems arrived in waves, from around the lake as well as from as far away as New Zealand. They became *Amethyst and Agate, solglimt*, reflections on Lake Superior.

These poems are often grounded in specific places: Grand Portage, Presque Isle Park, Miners Beach, Misery Bay, Copper Harbor, Little Spirit Tree, Hawk Ridge. Some reach back into the past, recounting the history of settlement around the lake—all the history you could taste in the water of Lake Superior: "iron ore in the bowels of the *Edmund Fitzgerald,*/the smell of Norwegian pancakes/from a cabin on the shore of Isle Royale in 1927. . ." as James Armstrong enumerates in "Oligotrophic." Some tell specific stories, like Heid Erdrich's "Gitche Onigaming, Grand Portage." Others focus on the people who forged the human history: the *Anishinaabe* voyageurs, miners, fishermen, Finnish workers gathered at the Koitto boarding house, welders, women and men in the joy and challenge of their daily lives.

Like those who live near the lake, these poems keep a close watch on the seasons and the sky: "My only conversation, the weather..." Morgan Grayce Willow declares. People of the lake know "late/ autumn yearns for a song/it will never hear again" as Kenneth Pobo writes in "Apostle Fall." There is a unique eloquence when considering winter: Terry Falsani's "blue clarity of zero, "Linda Glaser's ice—"frozen piles. . . [of] singing turquoise."

Many of these poets focus on the water itself: "the diamonds/ and silk of Superior" as Gary Boelhower writes in "After Sailing." Like painters, they draw on its palette of colors: amethyst, emerald, turquoise, sapphire, silver. Gwen Hart etches the sunset, "setting the water on fire" at Copper Harbor. Cecilia Lieder recreates an Easter dawn where "the sun flares out/song flowing upward ... resurrection." They capture the lick and thunder of waves crashing on bedrock. The fog and longing of the horizon.

Other poets are beachcombers, eyes focused on the shoreline—collectors of driftwood and feathers, agates, hematite, oolitic jasper, seaglass, bones. Not only treasures wash ashore, though, as Amy Jo Swing catalogs an afternoon's find: red plastic ribbon, a bicycle seat, a carburetor—evidence of the danger that humans can be to the lake. In "Temperance 2020," Susan Perala-Dewey demands we "see below the surface of our actions" and address "the steel barrels [that] sit in your belly/Waiting to explode with atomic #15—yellow phosphorus..." "How do we translate the flashing fins of poisoned fish?" Kimberly Blaeser asks in "Eloquence of Earth," "What other alphabet do you know to spell *contaminated waters*?"

Our health, our fate, our sense of wholeness are intricately connected to this lake. It calls us home—home to some specific beach, rocky shore, horizon. Home to ourselves. Deborah Cooper helps us hear that "primordial heartbeat/of the waves/a pulse that echoes/through my veins/ sews me back/into my own skin."

Lake Superior. "No pearls here, no shells to hold/to your ear to hear secrets," Ellie Schoenfeld writes in "An Unrefined Northern Metaphor," "This is not an/elegant well-behaved place." True. But how it has sung to these poets—and how they have resounded—keepers of the water, transcribers of that song.

Pamela Mittlefehldt
May 2015

GICHIGAMI

Dan Campion

Shark-visaged—don't trust me, go check the map—
Superior could scarf down Paumanok,
could swallow-whole Key Largo and Key West.
That's just in outline. Fleshed-out version means
you don your mask and dive where Longfellow
had no license to go: the freighters drowned,
the icecap's gouge, the sludge of modern use.
And while you're down there, wave and wind and sun
remake the picture-perfect topside lake
that painters paint and minnows navigate,
which, expert now, you can't appreciate;
it's just a landscape, water, skinny shore,
a play of light on surface, nothing more,
like Mississippi River to Mark Twain
when pilot training de-romanced that stream.
Except, of course, he had the memory still
of fresh eyes' first impression, of that thrill
Lucretius says we'll feel, observing stars,
by feigning we have not seen sky before.
It helps to tell a story: A great lake
much larger than Superior once rolled
to north and west. Glacial Lake Agassiz,
the dons called it, naming it for a don.

Superior and Agassiz, comrades
unvexed by humans, giants in deep time—
but you know this story, how one friend wastes,
dies, passes into other forms, is mourned
until new interests measure out relief.
No need to call in willing disbelief
when lake with lost companion, famished, scarred,
is of our kind, shark, mimic, mourner, bard.

SOLSTICE

Angela Ahlgren

The rocky northern shore
of Lake Superior
cuts Duluth diagonally and
from any intersection in Lakeside
I can see lake to the south
and lake to the east.

That's on a clear day.

Today white fog seals me in.
Lilacs hang, heavy jewels on black branches,
tall pines scratch the sky
peonies stand poised for ants to eat them open
to help them explode into a hot pink mess.

Maybe next week.

Today it's forty-seven degrees,
the longest day of the year.

I can see my breath
but I can't
see
the sun.

At the Koitto Boarding House, 1947

Angela Ahlgren

For my grandmother, Aura Rachel Maki

She likes the look
of the long table
its knots and lines
like abstract art
under a layer
of clear lacquer.
She sets out salt,
butter, jugs of milk
at even intervals.
She likes things neat.

She fills bowls
with mounds
of oatmeal, smooth
peeled eggs, bacon.
Food for hungry
men whose hands
work rope and steel
and ore, their
nails still black
after a scrub with soap.

Doors open, a rush
of boots and plaid
and stubble. Benches
scrape the floor.
Thirty arms reach,
tin plates fill, cups
of coffee steam.
At the corners
her mouth lifts
in a tiny smile.

She thinks of
pigs on the farm
in Humppila
noisy as they ate
troughs emptied
as soon as she
set them out—
but here, silence
with the meal, fuel
for a ten-hour shift.

She watches him,
ice blue eyes and
leather skin dark
from work in the
northern sun. He
fills his bowl
with oatmeal
sinks four boiled eggs
right into the middle.

Coffee black.

She likes his scar
a perfect line
down the center
of his bottom lip.
Knife fight, he
said once, when
he caught her gaze
but she knew
from his eyes
he was joking.

When the last
hunk of bread
is eaten
and the last
cup of coffee
gulped
she runs her rag
over the table
its imperfections
like Braille
beneath her fingers.

This poem is inspired by my maternal grandmother's stories of working at the Koitto Boarding House in Duluth, Minnesota in her twenties, after spending nineteen years living on a family farm in Finland. The Koitto Boarding House was located in an immigrant neighborhood once known as Finn Town and which is now Canal Park.

OLIGOTROPHIC

James Armstrong

Dead. Cold. Clear
as air. Pure
as ice: it takes180 years
for water to leave this basin,
which means—
says the limnologist on the radio—
if your nose were fine enough,
you could draw a cup and taste the musketry
of 1812, the ashes of Toronto.
The lake remembers more than we do:
blood rinsed from a tomahawk,
carbon from the Cloquet fire,
iron ore in the bowels of the *Edmund Fitzgerald*,
the smell of Norwegian pancakes
from a cabin on the shore of Isle Royale in 1927;
the acrid taste of taconite,
the stink of bloated lake trout, stench of burning
pyramids of sturgeon. Potato peels
from Louis Agassiz's Harvard expedition
in 1845. The heel of a moccasin
awash in Two Harbors
in the McKinley administration.

The webbed feet of a fish duck
at the mouth of the Big Two Hearted
River, right now, paddling.
A beer bottle tossed
from a party barge last night
in Murray Bay. Sawdust
from the last great white pines
on Grand Island
logged in the 1960s
and ferried across, section by section,
on this very lumber tug
tied to the dock
and leaking diesel.

WINDBOUND WITH DOSTOEVSKY

Milton J. Bates

June 2012

When Duluth flooded and zoo animals
drowned, the polar bear escaped. Before it
fell to a drug-tipped dart, it gave city folk
the *frisson* of a wilder place. The storm,
undarted, lumbered north and east across
the big lake, where it caught up with us.

We beached our kayaks and pitched our tent,
then rolled into fetal balls and played dead.
All night the thunder growled and lightning
clawed the sky. The worst of it was gone
by morning, hunting other prey. We woke
to the soft chatter of rain on nylon.

What better time for Dostoevsky?
All day his story of Muishkin, the gentle
prince misnamed The Idiot, unfolded
in our tent. When the rain stopped I took it
with me to the shore. Did stone and water
care that Nastasia lay dead in the ruins
of her wedding dress? That Rogojin
would do hard labor for her murder?

That the prince was once again an infant?

Superior still churned when I closed the book,
as though trying to scrub the human pain
from granite walls. Would they be clean by morning?
If so, the lake might have us back. We'd rise
refreshed, illiterate as serfs, and paddle on.

COUNTERPOINT

Samuel Black

When next I write a fugue,
I'll start with a large body of water,
seamless and innocent as any first theme.

In the responding second voice,
I'll sound the lake as deeper than before.
Ripples spawn melodies near the surface;
both voices interweave, waving.

With the third entrance, I'll invert the wave,
deftly rejoicing, reversing, the innocence.
New heights reveal new depths;
impassioned phrases expose sustained calm,
a trio of voices no longer separable.

As the bass emerges from below,
I'll nuture the voices toward intimacy.
Together, the waves they create
Hint—no—resound with undisclosed joys:
as when the dim-eyed fish and sunken vessels
sense the caress from a strumming lighthouse.

SLIPPAGE

Kimberly Blaeser

How many times lost
in the apparitions
of white dragon breath,
moon slipping in and out
behind the dancing fringe of fog?
Somewhere on the water's edge
trapped in the thin horizon line
between dark-sky Thunderbirds
and legendary spiked sea serpents,
lonely souls yearn or keen
on too solid ground.
Finding the vaporous shore
where every solid thing
becomes unseen,
where water fills air,
and the great panther still roars
against the rocks.
Mishibijiw
summoner of the storms,
your tail a vision like copper,
riding the seiche and surge
sinking us, jagged and heavy as rock,
in the uncanny call of night.

Three quadrillion gallons of water—
never enough for escape.
Your lair deep, deeper. . .
1,333 icy deepest feet down,
past lost schooners, sunken freighters,
in the miasma of myth
where the *Emperor* and the *Edmund Fitzgerald*
now waltz together sweetly
in currents of *Gichigami*.
Each lost legend summoned
swallowed like the *Nelson*.
Somewhere submerged, ship wheels still
then turn, the memory of squalls
brings splash and hiss echoing to shore
to wash the feet of wayfarers.
Who knows the lull and longing?
This ancient scented language
is sand, shells, and spray
the call of sea gulls and mystery,
is underwater monsters, craggy cliffs,
and, yes, our many drowned kingdoms.

ELOQUENCE OF EARTH

Kimberly Blaeser

Nominal signs, these words we use—*future, ecology, seven generations*—
have yellowed into clichés, editorials that line the cages
of captured birds, burn in unransomed stone fireplaces
of America's aspiring, royal mining families.
These green futures cast as fairy story,
sealed beneath the calloused ideals of legislators—
sleek smiling handshakes who seal bargains like Jabez Stone;
Our *I-do-solemnly-swear* paper-promise leaders
enticed by industry frenzy, slight of lips,
the short-sighted tally (seven hundred jobs)
coveted like Stone's seven years of prosperity.
Though publically professed (*against all enemies, foreign and domestic*),
and leather-oath sworn (*will bear true faith and allegiance*),
still *quid pro quos* reign, sell the soul of this land—
our waters our *manoomin* our children, *abiinoojiihnyag.*
Each season gavels strike new bargains with our oldest enemies
maji-manidoog, handsome fast-talking strangers disguised as prosperity.

Daily we watch patient warnings swim the Wolf River,
wash up on the shores of our great lakes,
migrate to absent wetlands, trumpet old calls.
How do we translate the flashing fins of poisoned fish?
What other alphabet do you know to spell *contaminated waters*?

Like banned books words still burn on my tongue—*reciprocity,*
sacred, preservation, earth, tradition, knowledge, protect.
Even the vellum of *justice* disdained, crumbled in quick greedy fists.
Meanwhile we gather here, descendants of *ajijaak* and *maang*
lift our ancient clan voices in longing, for a chant of restoration
in a Faustian world.

If I say *Gichigami—Lake Superior—a turquoise plain, stretches*
infinite, gete-gaming. If I say *Wiikonigoyaang, she invites us to her feast,*
how many will remember the eloquence of earth itself?
At dawn when *jiibay* mist backstrokes across the copper
of northern prairies eerie white hovering, damp and alive,
will you stretch out your hands in hope
cup the sacred like cedar smoke,
draw it toward you—a gesture
fervent and older than language?
Now I say *wiigwaasikaa,* everywhere we look
there are many white birch,
bark marked with sign, scrolls a history.
I say *ritual, continuum, cycle of belonging,*
I say *daga,* please; *ninandotaan,*
you must listen for it—*aki.*
Yes, our very earth speaks.
Who among us will translate?

After Sailing

Gary Boelhower

After sailing all day
through the diamonds
and silk of Superior,
the rhythm of the waves
still in my body, I dream
the wind sings in my bones,
hollow flutes for a symphony
of luster and I am

nothing

solid, stationary, past,
but permeable and empty
of everything but breath
pulled in and out by the moon.
The soul of the world shines
everywhere and even the green
hills on the shore are wave
after wave of sibilant light.

I am easily confused
about things of importance now.
I count my deepest obligations

to gardens, trails, silence.
I follow the wind's paws
on the blue water to catch
a final puff of breeze before turning
the bow toward the harbor. I am

nothing

but skin and bits of grape,
the dregs of intoxication.

Dance at Dawn

Gary Boelhower

Go out as far as you can
to sit alone on a stone throne
where you give up all the straight lines of your mind
in the dark quiet shiver an hour before dawn.
Set your eyes on that seam where water and sky
are stitched together in their great meeting
and when the fierce light tears the world wide
open for another day
dare to say your name
over the buckle and swell of waves
one sweet syllable of imperfect love
dare to say your name
not proud but in full voice
unfastened from any small hopes or pains.
Send it free as a smooth stone
skipping on the hammered blue
its singular dance
glancing gold in the new light
for a bright brief breath.

THE NORTH
(AFTER BORGES)

Jeffrey D. Boldt

To know the extremes of the seasons,
the no-illusions beauty of black
trees in January that will change at last,
just as the gray days become too heavy
to bear, into the lush cool lushness
of a northern spring...the tundra now meadow.

To attempt a wade in the sweet water sea,
Superior, in summer—to feel the grandeur
of spirit too big and cold for flesh.
To sip cognac on a pink lake
in mid-winter, or see a blue bird in May
that has flown all the way back from Brazil.
This, too, part of the poem.

Angling for Whitefish

Taina Maki Chahal

By 1920
the rainforest of fish
inland sea of pale-green
brown-backed deer of the Lakes
—Whitefish—
was exhausted. Yet,

before the settlers,
Whitefish, ancient underwater
understory of the forest of water
swam and swam
in a never-ending cycle,
collecting wisdom in
the hump on her back.

Sister of Salmon swam
in the underwater bountiful
Her nine kilos of silvery scales
flashed white
in a slow dance
above dark stones.

Seeking cold silence in summer,

Great Great Grandmother
Ancestor Atikameg
swam along the glacial depths
until Freezing Moon called then
She returned to swim
one eye closer to sky.

Circling through the seasons,
Ancestor Deer
collected great age
and animal wisdom,
storing her medicine in
the hump on her back.

Then came the captain
of commerce from Chicago
with his nets of profit
and offers of jobs—
for hungry settlers, that is.

In a language
that had no sacred grammar for
Ancestor Atikameg,
newsboys on Cumberland Street
cried "Free Trade!" even before
the term was invented by
neo-cons in the 1980s.

Whatever the term,
the terms are clear:

The captains of industry
fished out the forest
cut down the 800-year-old Ancestors
swimming in the glacial waters
at the bottom of Lake Superior.

Above,
the Thunderbirds
circled.

The Ice is Coming in like an Animal to the Shore

Sharon Chmielarz

like a brown skate skittering
through shallow water, fanning over
the lake's surface

and seal-like, too,
hunched on a rock
with other, washed-up seal-ice

dog-like, it
delivers past months in splinters,
nose pointing
with a scud missile's
straight-ahead precision

or a sea monster
streaking toward shore.
Its terrible,
wonderful,
glass voice
grates the lake

the lake in early spring,
a vellum covering,
the shoreline,
open water,
the ice.
The wild boar wind

rips the lake's seams into wounds, leaving a trail
of sooty-blue, narrow,
v-shaped crevasses
while over in the already
opened bay an aftermath of clam-blue ice
floats like lotus.

SAILING IN THE MOON'S WAKE

David R. Clowers

I know the difference
to sailors night makes

when moonlight hammers
Lake Superior's waves
into rough silver
sailing alone on luminous seas
like these
transforms this world

for now from waves
folding like linen off
the curve of my bow
Venus is born
and she sings
in the water caressing
the sides of my hull

Surprise me.

AFTER MATTHEW ARNOLD'S "DOVER BEACH"

David R. Clowers

We don't need metaphors to stand here
facing wind and Lake Superior's waves
that change our beach from day to day
and from year to passing year.

Where we are is the same as Dover's beach
and the water that grips our feet, and pulls
at us with sandy hands, is like the rip of a tide,
that flows to depths that are far beyond our reach.

And while we watch, a tern begins to hover.
When we join hands I begin to wonder
if we are as transient as these waves
and this bird who rides them like a lover.

In Dreams

Carolyn Colburn

In dreams when I'm not here, I see
this green, this sky, this air. I watch
my feet along this path, following
bunchberry down to the water, where
no things matter, save dragonflies
black and copper.

It seems we choose at every turn our own
way home. When I sit idling at a light
on 53, a crow stalking along the shoulder
eyes me. I hear not radios then, but ravens,
how they called on and off for days,
and I was there.

A hawk screams. It's June. Wildflowers
sprawl in a haze beyond the door, yellow
and blue. In January, shadow behind me,
I count tracks in snow—*deer, wolf, hare*—
feed chickadees and the fire, and no desire
for more. If one day I should go,

you will know where to find me.

ACROSS THE BORDER

Deborah Cooper

I've come to Canada
in search of something
I've lost hold of

something essential,
slipped away.

Its absence
in the hollow
of my throat

the ghost beneath
the breastbone.

Here, traces
of a scent
caught in the breeze

awake a stirring
at the farthest reach
of memory.

The giant,
sleeping still,
as in my childhood.

The giant's dreams,
still carried by the waves

carried away
in all directions.

Standing high above the lake,
heart-stopping drop
of cliff

and far below,
primordial heartbeat
of the waves

a pulse that echoes
through my veins

sews me back
into my own skin.

In Canada
I sleep
in my childhood's posture

arms open,
wide as wings.

In Canada
I dream again
of trees

of ancient secrets,
lifted in the breeze

whispered
in the drumbeat
of the waves.

The leaves and the lake
speak with the same voice

the same wind,
stirring the same songs

through the trees
and through the waters

and in all our depths
and limbs

a breath that never ends
begins again,
begins.

AFTER ALL OF MY LIFE

Florence Chard Dacey

Such a symphony of wind in trees
and boom of waves this morning after
thunder, rain. I want to climb
the unfurling birch tree and leap, without thinking.
I want to curl into the cobalt barrel
of the wave and release against these shores.

Such a talking to my face, the truth
of what it means to live here, die here
in each other's company.
Make everything move, make
this old heart and mind shake
this morning after all of my life
I've moved through like a mole,
like a wild turkey lost on the highway.

This is the magic world I never meant to leave.
The lichens are my first sturdy friends and they are many.
Graceful sticks rest across delicate blue flowers
and the dried black flies flutter somehow gaily too, in the web.
My body is a simpler heaviness
on the fire of ancient rock.
My spirit trembles like hidden seeds.

Superior at the Shoreline: February

Norita Dittberner-Jax

Think of it as a kingdom of ice,
its vast depths, turbulence in check,
the beach you walked,
the red umbrella you planted
in the sand, lost.

But find a spot, dig your boots
into the snowpack. Bring the quiet
you kept while the baby
slept, that cathedral silence.
Watch the lake begin to breathe
at the seams, the slight rise and fall
of its breast, the deep push
against ice, the first crack.

It will be weeks before it gains
strength at the shoreline to blast
the rocks on which you stood as a girl,
stunned by its fierce rhythm,
in love with it, as young girls love
the galloping horse.

LEVITATING TOWARD DULUTH

Norita Dittberner-Jax

I watch for the first pine, a flag of the country ahead,
and listen for the knock of geography shifting gears,
land rising out of bedrock and farm field.

Everything around me appears ordinary,
but inside I am waiting to be conducted
through something grand.

We climb higher, a long string of cars
crossing the St. Louis River, cutting through
the last elevation, then on to the top.

Suddenly the lake, huge and primal,
hidden behind the hunched shoulders of the hills
and with it the ships, bridges, and railroads,

all the commerce of water and land.
For a split second, we shimmer like trout
in the great flow of it, each bay and pier,

then shoot downhill into the stone channels
of the freeway, all our climbing released,
and arrive on the other side

of the city and onto the North Shore,
quiet now, we are inside geography,
we hum along, a string of cars

whose passengers turn naturally
to the thin line between water and sky
where all our hopes gather.

Water Colors

Deborah H. Doolittle

I paint with river water:
      a simple vase,
      a single rose.

I dip my brush in
      Missouri yellow,
      Rio Grande red,
      San Joaquin green.

The paper dimples, curls
with each brush stroke.

I paint the background Lake Superior.

The pigments settle;
the colors dry more naturally.

My still life runs,
      evaporates,
      leaves stones.

Wishing for Lake Superior

Deborah H. Doolittle

In the summer time, when the ferries
took us out to the islands
and the loons dove and laughed in our wake,
that is where I'd like to be.

Or, more importantly, when I'd like
to be, which was seventeen
and Duluth, the big city with shops
and bars I wanted to visit,

was across the state line and one year
in my future. We had packed
our hopes and fears along with our gear,
camped within sight of the shore,

cooked huge one-pot meals on the campfire
and snuggled deep in our tent,
watching the Big Dipper slowly turn
in the screen vents over our heads.

With the transistor radio tuned
to whatever rock and roll
station with a strong enough signal,
we'd sing along with the songs

and eat blueberries and Oreos.
We'd made plans for the future
we thought we could see as clearly as
the bright beams from our flashlights.

That summertime, when each single day
inched its slow way into night,
and then another day, with nothing
better to do than remember.

FREIGHTERS SLIDE BY

Barbara Draper

Quietly, either you see them or you don't—
freighters slide by like ghosts, long dashes—

tracing the horizon from north to south.
Call them the continuum of the unseen.

Lie yourself down on the beach and ride that freighter
across the rim of the horizon—

your only chance with this one hour:
be the whitefish stirring up waves,

be the beach grass, wind-whipped, slender and yielding,
building a house of sand,

be the eagle just landed on a rock,
a stone's throw away, the water splashing over his talons,
washing his feet,

be the man you can't see on the ore boat, leaning on the rail,
watching the endless churn of water peeling
away from the stern,

the three old women, familiar,
paddling an ash canoe,

the soul on a lark, time uncorked
the sideways sounds of water.

GITCHE ONIGAMING,
GRAND PORTAGE

Heid E. Erdrich

Here is the path my people walked
hauling immense trade canoes,
the semi-truck of centuries past.

Here between Great Lake and Great North,
earth curves visibly toward the arctic ice
that now flows in places never open before.

Here guests can hear a natural history
of the beaver, gold standard for
a century of trade from isle to inland.

Here re-enactments and regalia
keep history current, preserve trappers'
ways, traders' wares, all the era conveys.

Here ghostly silver warehouses of bare wood,
a portage path eight and a half miles:
full of meaning, necessary, contested.

Here a National Monument arose by
Presidential declaration to urgently protect
Gitche Onigaming's place in time.

Here begins North and territories beyond,
where ice opens a passage that, a century past,
would have made this path unnecessary, unprotected.

There the true path, the mark, the monumental.

Manidoo Giizhikens: Little Spirit Cedar Tree

Heid E. Erdrich

Who makes a shawl of her own arms

Who wraps herself up
holding the last warmth
of someone she loved once
one hundred or two hundred or seven hundred years since

We lift our faces to her many faces

Whose hair frights and stands into the wind
terrified or terrifying
we only know when close
how to take her pose
which changes as women change
day by day by day

We lift our faces to her many faces
We hold our bodies to her many bodies

Whose way with wind makes a call
we must answer must slip on tilting rocks
pass between a boulder portal
to her side her knees her waist

We lift our faces to her many faces
We hold our bodies to her many bodies
We give our voices to her many voices

We fall to her in our need
to breathe her astringency
her cleansing medicine

We lift our faces to her many faces
We hold our bodies to her many bodies
We give our voices to her many voices
We gift sweetgrass asema stones tokens

We take away no sureness of her
aware only that time whirls waves
makes bone-bleached sculptures of us all

We do not believe that she is small
she who brinks the greatness of creation,
the greatness of the lake while tied to rock
grown small in spirit maybe but no
she holds stone to stone she composes the cliff
We know her then we do not know her

We hold our bodies to her many bodies
We give our voices to her many voices

Whose tortured form twists
away at once and ever back
her pain an emblem of release

she gives over to the waves
waves that change as she changes
one day gray the next vivid as prism

We give our voices to her many voices
We gift sweetgrass asema stones tokens

Whose torso blown with holes
suffers no loss but fills
her crevices sensual as pleasure
etched with florescence of lichen
She hides and shows at once
She chooses all and gives all away

We hold our bodies to her many bodies
We lift our faces to her many faces

And this is why the painter
addresses her for fifty years
sees her new in every light
Every hour on every day a year can make

We lift our faces to her many faces
she returns a thousand forms
and we have been every one of them

We lift our faces to her many faces and she remains

WOODED ROAD, LAKE SUPERIOR

Michelle Bonczek Evory

When we pass an opening, a keyhole
through which waves break and scatter
pebbles like rock candy slammed into rock,

he stops the car. Even I hear it calling.
It is a beautiful evening, the sun,
the horizon. Give me the keys,

I say, in case something happens, in case
his body, too supple for these waves,
all flesh and bone, a nymph of a body

scarred by old rebellion and blades, is swallowed
by these forces that command him to swim.
I know I cannot compete with nature.

He heeds to the water, as we all will one day,
I say to myself, strolling the beach, praying—yes,
with him I have returned to prayer—give me

strength to leave him be. These waves, tortured
by their yearning to unhinge,
rap the bottom of cold, shipwrecked depths.

I've plunged and carried an ache for days.
He tosses his clothes. First feet and already
his body is thrown back. I hide calm

behind my camera, take a few pictures of him
inching into the lake, for the caretakers,
I think, should they need come—which will be me

on this stretch of land too far north for tourists
or towns. But stones and water hear as well as call.
They cut deep into his right foot. He will notice

the blood only when he changes
into his clothes and walks back, on second thought,
the wet sand sucking sunsets from his heel.

LAKE SUPERIOR SPRING

Teresa Boyle Falsani

Below Skyline Drive, the land
the lake the land again the sky
lie layered in shades of ash,
like dusty Venetian blinds
shut for days against the sun.
Even the evergreens have gone gray,
ghosting like druids into the mist.

A tepid rain pocks at patches
of dirty snow, exposing
swaths of wrinkled earth
like skin too long bandaged,
bleached and bloodless.

This far past the equinox,
who would have thought I'd miss
frost etched on the window,
the blue clarity of zero?

THE WORK OF WATER

Teresa Boyle Falsani

There is up north a creek
tumbling helter-skelter over rocks
as sleek as a seal's back,
swollen with the sorrow of snow
melting too fast to evaporate.
Into this creek I once tossed sticks,
one after another, naming each.
This twig bears worry for my son,
a willow switch, my anger at a friend,
a thick oak branch for my father's pain,
peeling birch, my mother's bitter tears.
I watched them slip and slide
toward the great gray lake,
and wished it were that easy
to let pain go.

Years later, beneath a sun
too hot for snow,
I walk along the lakeshore
strewn with polished driftwood,
cobbled with smooth stones
tumbled by time

and weight of wave.
These are the relics
I gather now,
like the flash of my father's smile,
a call from a friend forgiven,
gifts of the work of water
to cradle in my bare hand.

CROSSING THE CONTINENTAL DIVIDE

Lynda Ferguson

My soul has again
been ripped in two
pulled apart at its seams
it feels like it is not possible
to stretch over this distance
between the place of my birth
and the birthplace of my child
my origins and my creations
two sets of family and friends
always waiting to embrace me

It happens every time I go
back to where I come from
my heart drumming around
up and down through black and gray,
red and white and golden buttes
deep ravines and alkaline gullies
cactus, sage, white cedar and cottonwood
pillowed quilts of paha sapa pine
fringed robes of buffalo grass swaying
deer and antelope playing hide-and-seek.

In the hollows, curves and pitted caves of
soft sandstone and hard limestone
there are traces of old rivers and
more recent torrents of thunderheads;
this mystic theater I am passing by
holds me eternally spellbound.
Seeing it in my rearview mirror,
I come undone; I force myself to
look away, far far ahead, and
lean heavily into the wind.

I cry my way back to the great lake
I ask her to mend me and she does.
Blankets of thick fog hold me until dawn;
sea smoke prayers give way to
turquoise, amethyst and sapphire waves,
soft warm sands and clear cool agates.
Through tall stands of jack pines, red cedars,
sweet sugar maples and peeling paper birches,
she sings of the connectedness of our Mino Aki...
the resilience of bonds, and the wholeness of me.

Voyageur

Phil Fitzpatrick

Alors, you stalwarts belting out
Alouette, you vagabonds Jacque
Marcel Pierre Louis at your work
painters Hopkins Jaques Sivertson
capture your lives and color in theirs
heroic bold so rough-and-tumble
wool cap leather boots and beard
your clay pipe sash your print shirt
baggy leggings that pirate getup
your private stories we know not
yet those of your lusty comrades
we have read and sung and told
utensils fabric beads and weaponry
countless drowned canoes fabled loads
across an infinity of portages
trading through the decades centuries
barter with industrious woodland bands
Assiniboine Athabascan Anishinabeg
Algonquin Cree trappers traders all

your watery milieu the Great Sea
her wide gray ominous expanse
her caps her breakers the drenching

cacophony of her thunderstorms
rocks of every conceivable origin
by Split Rock Pukaskwa and Red Cliff
the bluffs at Grand Portage where
you overwinter swapping tales tall
eating bannock salmon hash and gruel
swilling grog through the harsh dark
a restless wait for April's drip and flow
til up the surge of the winding Pigeon
again you paddle singing stroking
dreaming of the home you never see
your true home now just Gitchi Gumi

Lake Drought

Margot Fortunato Galt

Even on these rocks
usually under water,

scum whitens in the sun.
The lake lowers
another notch.

Burn off, disaster.
This is August,
common spoke on
the wheel to ice.

The king makes his
rounds, never blinks.

Praise heat, our
night will come.

*

If only we had stayed put,
stopped migration
in flaming cars,

not torched trees
to match the sun,

each decade sloughed
faster, snake
of our greed.

*

Now I wait
on dumb rocks
patient to the end.

Days I walk their gray flanks,
come home, hands
full of metal cans,
plastic cups,

my late bouquet
of small worries.

Northwestern Ontario

Julie Gard

Two days after the flood, we drove north with our aging rat terrier
and crossed into Canada. With the border guard's permission, he
peed between countries. The cancer was already growing under his
blue argyle harness. Lake Superior swelled by the highway, a swish
in my right ear, a honing pull. George sensed it with his nose in
the window crack, tracking geese to Thunder Bay.

I kept thinking of home, Lester River running so hard its banks
were stripped to rock, the sump pump going all night. Nipigon
was lovely yet resigned, the bad economy, the oddly stocked
stores, the gift shop owner who had just been punched. Hot tea
in clear glasses with the bay just beyond us and the dog in cracked
shade in the car.

In the provincial park, George crossed a waterfall and ran up
the trail to the top of his life. He stood in phlox, iris and tansy,
cataracts swimming with miles of lake. We let go of that dog when
we needed to, but first we took him to Canada, gave him all of the
water in the world.

"Breakwater 1" *by AJ Atwater*

"North Dakota Kayaks" *by Sue Pavlatos*

"View from Oberg Mountain" *by Alberta Marana*

"Superior Dawn" *by Cecilia Lieder*

"Temporal Display" *by Penny Perry*

"Untitled (Flow)" *by Sarah M. Brokke*

"Hidden Anchorage" *by Thomas Rauschenfels*

"At the Shore" *by Cecilia Lieder*

Watermark

Jane Graham George

Still uneasy with the move
from Fort Bragg to St. Paul,
we were camping our way north
toward Duluth and then on to Gooseberry Falls,
a day in early June, tropical at 9 a.m.,
with the station wagon window open,
we wagged our feet out from the rear-facing seat
and waved at every stranger we passed.

That was the first time,
somewhere near Cloquet
the smell of the lumber mill,
the land rising slow as a bear
from winter slumber,
and there at the top
was the lake, shimmering,
a distance of forever
to my 12-year-old eyes.

Many times over the trip repeated,
orange lichen on bedrock,
at Paradise Beach ice shards in winter,
agates and pink thomsonite in summer,

the Spirit Tree Cedar and a shipwreck
on the way to Isle Royale,
the names and places,
snow melting on Baptism River,
Split Rock Lighthouse,
Tettegouche, Cascade River.

Even once, far from the lake,
somewhere in Los Angeles,
was it City of Industry or Carson or
maybe San Pedro, near the Pacific,
I came upon a 200-yard length
of roofing iron and thought
it was the lake,
blue-grey as a heron.

The mind imprints what it loves.

So today from the southern tip
of the north island of New Zealand,
a silvery mist-heavy day,
I see it again, the broadest expanse
I had ever known as a child,
teeming here with salmon and herring,
blue whales even heading to the Southern Ocean,
saltwater version of my Great Lake.

Wellington, New Zealand

CROSSING OVER

Candace Ginsberg

Still
cold
and in the distance
across the grey blue waters
the horizon has blurred—
melded with the winter dark.

And crossing that divide
a lone long ship
with its warm cabin lights
reveals the path it travels
while another, its mere reflection,
marks the place
and space
it has left behind.

THE GREAT LAKE

Linda Glaser

In winter
it is another world.

Come.
Step off the frozen ground.

Place your feet
on this rock-solid body
of immense water—
sturdy and vast enough
to make you feel safe
small
insignificant.

Come.
Walk on this other land
where great slabs of ice
lie belly up—
throwing bright shafts
and blinding memories
of a closer warmer sun,

frozen piles
too heavy to budge
yet scattered like pebbles
and singing turquoise—if you're lucky.

Walk above
uncountable lives
orbiting deep below winter—
kindred miracles
of eyes and gills
breathing their own universe,
swallowing
light and darkness.

Feel how this shining world
magnifies the sky
the quiet
the wild

Savor
this vast unrelenting cold
and how immensely good—
soon
soon
to be
back indoors
cradling all this
inside you.

NIGHT SKY

Tom Hansen

We see it always
as if for the first time—
the great inverted bowl of the sky
poked full of holes letting light leak in
from the other side we are forbidden to see.

Something inside us is chilled by that desert,
that black shoreless ocean of night,
but something is warmed
by stars beyond number—
all those pinpricks of cold tiny light.

And standing here on this North Shore pier
gazing down into black placid water,
we see them swaying—
stars on the wide sleeping
face of Superior.

MESSAGES

Gwen Hart

I cannot understand the language
of sand, prefixes and suffixes constantly
shifting, adhering and falling away
from the white tongues of the breakers.

All day, I watch the great ships
lumber like slow actors, forgetting
and remembering their lines
in the fog off Misery Bay.

The cottonwoods let down their
white seeds at Presque Isle Park,
forming new constellations
in the grass around our feet.

While we walk at Miner's Beach,
Petoskey stones rattle in my pocket,
narrating each step with their chatter
about the coral of long-forgotten seas.

There is no instruction manual
for setting the water on fire
the way the sun does every evening
at Copper Harbor.

A loon wets its dark beak
in the Mouth of the Huron
and writes a story
only the wind can read.

After Forty-Three Years

Mara Kirk Hart

For Lake Superior

I can't deny, at first I was bewitched
You're beautiful, but rough around the edges
You think you're such a big shot, always bragging
"The biggest and the deepest and the cleanest."

But now a lot about you bothers me:
Communication's always been a problem
You groan and hiss and never can be silent
You're untrustworthy, unreliable
You promise picnics, then you're gray and sullen
And sometimes downright mean: you've cut and bruised me
Your temper's bad, your disposition's cold
And still, you think you're, well, Superior.

My old boyfriend back east beguiles me still:
He's smooth around the edges, soft and fine
You're right, he can be stormy too, like you
His spirits sometimes high and sometimes low
But unlike you, he never lets me down
He buoys me up when I am feeling blue
His tears are salty, as tears ought to be
He's my first love; I'm tempted to return.

Gooseberry Falls, Duluth, Minnesota

Susan Carol Hauser

It is not much comfort—to think
of you at sea, returned
to the water, or the air,

whatever that land is
that we seem to come from.

It is hard, though, to not
indulge in metaphor:

the rivers of our blood
returning again and again
to the heart;

rain, snow, mist,
even ice returning again
and again to the ocean.

I turn to water, then,
to waterfalls,
on this the anniversary
of your passing, perhaps

with hope of finding you,
falling into grace,
into the quiet water
that down the way nudges
into Lake Superior, resisting
the waves that resist the current,

where I skip stones,
small memories,
and pocket one pebble
for when I am lost,
as though at sea.

LAKE SUPERIOR

Susan Hawkinson

When we played in the Big Lake, we swam close to each other.
  Tumbling like otters under and over,
      we shrieked,
            splashed,
                  climbed thigh
                        to hip
                              to shoulder.
Palms together, arms raised, steeples rising above the waves,
    we flung ourselves headfirst into our reflections,
        shattering our images,
                as we dove toward the sunlit ridges of sand.
Eyes open to what lay ahead,
          no masks—no gear—
    Lake Superior, take us back there:
                Let me grab your feet and bounce you, lounging
                    like a raft on the water.
                Let me make waves out of your body.
                Let me roll you and roll you until, like a top,
                    careening toward the outcrop,
                          you scale the jagged rocks.
          I follow you up the footholds
                where you wrap me like a mummy
                    in your wet towel.

You say,

I can swim you to the harbor in this cold water—

if you keep your hands on my shoulders.

I say,

I want risk—not rescue.

Let's swim forever.

Diving in,

    my skinny arms work hard while your strong shoulders glide

        through the water like a muskrat,

    as if some small engine powers you along,

        carving our fame like Ulysses onto the watery world.

Big Lake and sky,

    waves and light,

        let the world wait—

            yes wait—

      while we refuse

          all calls from shore.

I TELL THE LAKE A STORY

Eva Hooker

How its gray is made

Out of shadow and disturbance.

And green and blue: dark round circles of stone.

How sun falls through without harness. Torrential.

All body work.

How it turns its hand.

Writes in leading strings

Of wild.

How I turn my face.

Read its deep ground, alluvial.

Its umber mouth.

How the rain hums out there.

Sudden, white and yellow gold like fields of late wheat.

I must take shelter.

How the mergansers gather and talk to themselves.

Wash their feathers in preparation

For winter ghost-walking.

Afterward, the lupine seeds

Fall from their furled fur.

The black cat waits for me

At water's edge.

She says, come, come and look.

I tell her how I know

In August my heart has passed over

To where fullness hangs

Suspended like the round moon.

How my hand-lines spell.

My fingers could not stop flowering

In purple lavender.

Out of nowhere how I gathered

Everything I could see and laved it

Over myself. I said, yes.

The lake is stirring.

I have passed over to where there is no other

House. The humming-

Bird dives into the sea-roses and lifts

Her body. How then, the sun falls fluent

In wide flares of red fire. Panging—

How I watch.

THERE IS WORK TO DO WITHIN NOTHINGNESS

Eva Hooker

A simple solitude: slow light seams the land. The great bird turns upon the thermal. Its aloneness, unrestrained, fiercely elegant. It knows no shallow places. It cannot hold back.

> Even its smallest feathers hook the air.

The lake keeps watch for the legible footprint of matter. I worry to move over it and slip my paddle in, let the water fold back upon itself. The curve of falling water demands something of us we had not perceived.

> We write by hand.

My hand mars the heart-gray surface. It scatters the admissible. Someone said *Ruin is formal.* White linen, necessary. Also, the collapse

> Of beauty.

Its white head turning, its yellow eyes prepared for reading rooms made of water upright and edged. Where we land, loosestrife and pale anemone. All three of us locked deep in shadow and silt.

> *Which is the abler soul?*

Telling, telling parts of the heart, the lake breathes, hurries us, its foot on the treadle. My hand cannot hold what it contains.

We move in tidal wind.

The lake comes to fetch me to underwater work. Granite stones catch fire. I trace pools of light, watch a brown spider navigate the lake-skin. It walks as if on nothing.

Each step, intimate and careful and sheer.

Voyager travels between the stars.

Up there to know *what is between* is to know—

Yet, we are far, far outside. Vacant. Inscribed.
Ground-figures singing like they do in opera: Give me, give me back the night.

The great bird comes to rest in white pine. The sun sinks down through upturned branches.

Fretting the light.

Shadowfall. Where my hand was no longer is: *anima mundi.*

I leave no trace.

INTO ALL THINGS WE ENTER

Ann Iverson

Superior, ship-less
save one ghostly vessel
and one path of sun
towards a shore
beyond our knowing
a destination of light.

Seagulls not seen
or remembered
nor the passers-by
nor memory's intent.

Into all things we enter.
Into all things we become.
Into this calling
into this watery message.

This calm, this sane
on the verge of something
at the brink of brightness
of a land so emerald
you can hear it
gather at your feet.

Speaking to Lake Superior Elders

Janet Jerve

It is this lake that I long for
and yet these rocks,

elders of the earth,
are what hold me here.

Once molten mountains,
they are now slabs

ground down by glacial ice
left here after the melt of time.

Now the rim of the cup
of this beautiful lake,

these slabs send heat into my back
as I lie in the sun, listening

to the push and pull of waves,
eyes shut as I picture them rolling in:

white ruffled edges against the dark and deep blue,
reaching their mark, then digging down,

scooping stones in the rhythm of earth and moon,
back and forth, in and out,

the breath of the lake
the body of the lake inhaling, exhaling

until the rock itself and
the skins of the smaller stones below

are worn smooth as they rock
back and forth from the wear of daily life.

Ancient ones, what do you know
that you haven't yet told me?

Hawk Ridge

Jim Johnson

As September flies into October
the hawks fly south, out of the boreal
forests, out of the arctic, out of
the north, or what we know as north.
The hawks fly south, fly south
until the greatest of the great lakes
Lake Superior leers at them like the
head of a wolf. The wolf leering,
cold winds blowing, the hawks veer
down the shore, down the shore of the great lake,
hawk after hawk after hawk,
flights of hawks flying down the north shore
of Superior,
hawk after hawk after hawk
down the head of the lake. Then waiting,
waiting for the crossing of the great lake
the hawks gather,
circling above,
above and before the cold lake,
northern goshawk, cooper's hawk, and
sharp-shinned hawk,
hawks kettling above,
a fine kettling of hawks

stirring overhead
the way my grandmother stirred
her soup, her *mojakka* with a wooden spoon.
Once when I was a boy
barely tall enough to look into
the dented pot she was stirring, I saw two eyeballs
looking back at me, two eyeballs looking back
at me from the head of a northern pike
swimming in the stirred milk
as my grandmother hummed and tapped
her foot to a minor-keyed *hoijakka*
and stirred her soup with a wooden spoon.
I will never forget
two eyeballs looking back at me
as my grandmother stirred her soup.
Now the kettle of hawks
circling overhead,
stirred by the wind.
Hawk after hawk after hawk,
northern harrier, rough-legged and
white-tailed hawk,
hawks kettling overhead. The great wind
strumming through the trees as
hawk after hawk after hawk,
Swainson's, broad-winged, and red-shouldered
hawk after hawk after hawk
stirred by the wind,
kettling over the great wolf's snout,
kettling overhead, hawks
waiting for the wind to change

to a major key,
for the clouds to lift, then
the hawks rise up
hawk after hawk after hawk,
American kestrels, peregrine falcons, and hawks
hawks flying over the head of the wolf,
the great thermal lifting their wings out
and over the lake,
the hawks flying, the hawks flying south,
flying south, south of what we know.

AGATES

Meridel Kahl

Tumbled for epochs
along
wave-battered
shores,
these stones
speak of
lava runs
water rage
crawling ice
wind bite.

Circled round
in rings of light—
rust-orange
yellow
red—
glimpsed through
layers rugged with time,
these stones
seduce
with the shine
of Venus
in evening skies.

TO BEGIN AGAIN

Meridel Kahl

Just when
you see yourself
reflected against
a darkening world,
leaves dress
spring-shore trees
an otter bathes
on the belly
of a rock
a sailboat hangs
like a pendant pearl

waves
sing to you
in syllables
of sapphire
and silver.
as they take
you to a place
where water
meets sky
as they touch
each cell
in your body
with blue.

In Concert, the Fluency

Maggie Kazel

Colder than you are deep,
deeper than nearly all the others
your borders half city, half sky,
Lake, you are so superior,
the jazz in you sublime, discordant,
the gospel, a full shout of praise
every wave, and of course
there's rock 'n roll, of course!

But last and first
you embody the blues
of blues you know no shortage,
even, perhaps most in,
your icy reverie
that time when you sing
nothing but the 'No-one-knows-me-now' blues
and the 'I-threw-your-love-to-the-bottom-of-this-lake' blues
plus the always in demand
'If-ice-were-money-I'd-be-singin'-something-else-forever' blues
violent churning, steel knives cresting
the blues roiling, the blues rocking,
the blues incantation to the gods,
deliver us to the gods!

In summer, in samba,
no sign of need
for chest beating blues,
no grim grinding rock
no glare of ice
we shed our clothes,
we shift dance on your shores,
inspired foot work, fancy foot work,
light splintered and laughing all over your waves
these are the 'laid-out-bare-and-waiting' blues
the spell of your graces we trance on, want to climb in,
that calm, ecstatic silence, that absolute joy
in continuous concert,
your floating fluency
in bliss

Spirit Little Cedar
Grand Portage Reservation

Susan Deborah King

FOR HAZEL BELVO

Tree sacred to native people,
I see in you myself.
I too have grown up out of rock
with no visible nourishment
at my roots.
I twisted and turned gripping
what was hard, cold, unyielding—
all there was—
to straighten and raise
a modest, needled crown.
Struggle is ingrained in my sinews
as it is in your grooved bark.
While taller, ground-rooted trees
around you have been felled by storms,
you, for centuries, on a point,
alone and vulnerable,
have prevailed.
That is why I come.
Teach me, for the days left me,
how, as you seem to, to embody
movement in a pose.

Your trunk bends like river courses;
your branches lift like arms of one
dancing with abandon.
As you have been to many,
let me be a totem
for those who fear,
because of loss or lack, position or circumstance,
illness or harm done to them,
that they have no ground to stand on,
no conditions to encourage growth,
let them read in my story,
so as not to lose heart,
the oldest of all truths:
the Nothing is our mother
and the hollow out of which
all that has ever lived was born.

LATE ICE

Mary F. Lee

The beauty of what Winter brought;
a brazen slung belt for her lake-dazzled hips,
a shimmy of quartz composed of April melt,
thick with daggers, white, blue, and sharp
against the pleated mirror of Superior's gown
which sways and lifts those old lost ships
and the poor souls inside who spiraled down
then fell, at last, to sleep in its inky silk.
Rocking, rocking, the water lulls our eyes;
we droop upon the shoulder of our love
and rest inside the sleeve of the horizon.
Beneath our feet we almost can perceive,
in the winking light of the rock tossed shore,
all the silver buckles they once wore.

Easter Dawn on Superior

Cecilia Lieder

there will be no light
gray winter covers the sky
why do I persist?

black shoreline edges
laced with blinding neon ice
cold beauty starves breath

hidden dawn shreds clouds
with fiery trails of red light
pearls on lake ripple

cloud-fish swimming by
under-lit with burning white
ceaseless glowing waves

through a threadbare cloud
suddenly the sun flares out
song flowing upward

releasing all ties
ascent into unbounded peace
resurrection

SHOVEL POINT
Judy Lindberg

A grain of granite hangs on for years in strong wind
on this cliff high above Lake Superior.
Particles dissolve, a small pore forms,
another grain flies away and another
and another until millions leave
exposing a vein of milky quartz
along which the cliff will crack
into chunks.

————————————————

There's a clarity here.
Birch branches, maroon on blue sky,
thin pine needles, the white porcelain
tiles of the lighthouse.
My skin has the dry slipperiness
of the rocks I rub my hands over,
my fingernails scraping
stiff orange-black crusts of lichen,
lifting sheets of mica sunk
in surfaces. I split rocks open,
looking for smoothness within,
dark-lined agate or faceted crystals
of amethyst sticking out
like a stone forest.

A scrub pine grows on a pad of moss
near the edge, hanging on
by its bare roots pressed into fissures.
We saved our marriage in Pittsburgh
running from bar to bar one night.
Outside the Silver Fox we sat in the car.
I felt the roots we've sunk into each other
divide into soft shoots.

Below me are sharp-edged chunks
that have recently split
from the cliff and round rocks
that have rubbed each other smooth.
The lake echoes deep, sliding
the rock wall. I think of jumping
or falling off, of my hard old roots
slipping loose between eons.
I think of my childhood dreams
of expanding, leaving my body
and the temptation to go on
but returning. I wanted
that dream again, wanted
to keep it
as an option.

I come here often, imagining
the cold of the glacier
that shoveled this lake out,
imagining the bend of the earth where the water

meets the sky and the feel of the earth spinning.
I see the rise of lava in the curl of the cliff.
I walk old beach lines, imagining
boulders pounding down hills, settling in crevices.
And when I see the bone wings of a moose
rise in the woods, I am embarrassed of my fright.
His large eyes are dark and calm.

Key Sequences Missing

Micky McGilligan

There are no little shops to distract you here.
It is a dangerous place to live
full of violence and weather.
The clouds are so thick
a voice can barely penetrate them.
The only messages left are written on bread or melting snow.

Let me remind you.
Extreme caution is no longer an admirable quality.
Discretion, prudence, circumspection, foresight, vigilance.
These are liabilities when progress is bearing down on you.

It is embarrassing not to be able to find yourself in a crowd.
But maybe reaching the grocery store
maneuvering your way around the streets
is the best find to expect,
even with underlying hunger bottled within you.
If you want to send a message, you have to empty the bottle
and write a note defining the situation.
If you prefer not to be rescued,
break the bottle or let the waves do it for you.

LAKE SUPERIOR POEM

Lisa McKhann

FOR JESS

Some days, our great lake, Superior
with its deepest depths and broadest breadths
proves undersized and incapable
as a watershed, an international basin, of holding
even one woman's grief.

My young friend is failing here, along its western-most tip.
She and I walk or trot Superior's sand spit
the longest in the world
and six miles of beach have always been enough.

Standing puny on its shore, I know its best exposures.
Dark cliffs loom north, pummeled by storms
or warming in sunshine
to stake my anger in howling wind
or let it curl up and doze for a merciful minute
beside a tiny pool-side garden of moss and lichen
tucked into a bedrock niche
the vast expanse behind me, until on waking
vertigo, to have forgotten where I am.

Cobble beaches to rock hound,
boot heels grind down with a satisfying growl
stooped to look but don't look, that Zen thing
slow, open to what comes along,
there, bring it close, roll it this way, that
then chunk, lost again among the others or
pocketed for awhile. Maybe it's a keeper
an agate, a koan.

Just crossing the dunes is enough some days
with that downward drag while climbing a hill of sand
sliding, practically flailing, until bare feet reach the top
and I look up from them, feeling my heart in my chest
to behold, almost like religion, what vista is borne
across this body of water to me, today.

The walk along this small stretch of shore
changes with the slope, with how damp
or dry the sand, and what new coves and crescent shapes
have arrived on sculpting waves, even in summer
a good solid trudge.

She does her best, our Lady Superior, mother of freshwater.

One day, sand pipers skitter just ahead along the hem
of her skirt at water's edge, little running arcs
like embroidered stitches one step ahead of you
endearing and comical.

In winter, thick panes of ice form
jewels, castles, and all things magical
you hear before seeing, the gallumpf of an icy blow hole
where slush water shoves up from beneath to form
a smooth cone, that funny sound, glump glump.

Some days, among lake-sorted stones she gives me her best,
the rolled balls of duff and twigs—curious beach balls
of the humblest materials, offering
don't be sad or angry or furious.
See this silly thing I've rolled out of my depths
egg-shaped, seemingly fragile, but clearly not.
Don't fill your pockets with sadness.

I will walk, doze, and comb my way
some more and hope this reservoir
proves deep and varied enough for us all.
Today, I simply cannot believe in superlatives
in Superior and God. Not even in Art.

POET LAUREATE OF DULUTH

Pamela Mittlefehldt

The competition is fierce.
The sensuous swell of hills
curving around the city like a sated lover
on the cusp of rekindled desire—
        surely a touchstone for that latent creative fire.

The madcap jesters:
rivers and creeks leaping
        and
        somersaulting
as they tumble and spark their way
through glens and subdivisions,
past parking lots and pristine pines—
first choice for alliteration and dialectic analogy.

The gulls,
bawdy bards squalling their librettos,
squawking in counterpoint
to the trickster crows,
their cries onomatopoeia in motion.

But the laurel falls unanimously
on the Lake—

that capricious Muse
who takes your breath away
as you crest the hill
and are pierced by moonlight:
holy revery.

That restless energy that sails your dreams
        or drowns them.
Unfathomable, yet so intimate
her liquid tongue
flicks the arch of your foot.

Never daily.
She refuses any schedule—
will never flatter fools—
will not chant on demand
or wallow through another wrack
of bloated sonnets.
Neither patience nor praise
are in her lexicon.

But how she sings—
how she condenses sky, rain, dream
into one shining canto
of longing and mystery.

Breathing cloud and thunder,
her magic outstorms any cycle
of rhyme or rhapsody.

Our words are driftwood
tossed on the heat-baked shore,
the scrabbled calligraphy of our
stuttered lyrics
erased by one sighing wave.

Her silence sounds with metaphor and meaning.
We wait—wordless—
while she tongues the ledgerock,
makes it howl with joy.

Sailing Superior

Yvonne Pearson

The wind presses us forward,
Six knots per hour—or one.
Either way, progress is the thing.

Sunset is geometry: equidistant
yellow bars charted on the water,
float carelessly apart,

mutable geometry.
If the universe contains all things,
is it both mutable and immutable?

Are we still moving?

Apostles, more than twelve of them,
stand witness to the boundary between us.
This we knew before.

And the other thing we knew?
Bones lie deep beneath her surface.

TEMPERANCE 2020

Susan Perala-Dewey

Gitchi-gami, bring us your emerald light to bear
Allow us to see below the surface of our actions
Regain our sense of balance with the universe

Already the steel barrels sit in your belly
Waiting to explode with atomic #15—yellow phosphorus
"unsafe to handle without water . . . a small amount will cause
death"

Taconite Harbor tailings
Leach magnetite powder, poisoning lungs
Sifting and settling into mouths of bottom feeders

Already these heavy metals weigh you down
Silver mercury refines your rippled surface
Lines your ribs, heats your organs
Settles our bets on freshwater forever.

"Brighton Beach" *by Arna Rennan*

"Full Circle" *by Adam Swanson*

"Across the Border" *by Joel Cooper*

"Reflected Sea" *by Thomas Rauschenfels*

"Apostle Island Shore" *by Jan Wise*

"Sky and Life" *by Adam Swanson*

"Sea Creatures" *by Thomas Rauschenfels*

STOCKTON ISLAND

Kenneth Pobo

We walk to Presque Isle Point
on the tombolo, a mound
rising up out of Superior,
lake like an ice

snake. Singing sand,
the island solid in flux.
Soft water lilies in a bog,
some green, some reddening.
Boulders. People
lived here 3000 years ago.
What does someone who
endured such a winter
know about spring
that we don't?

Quarrymen unearthed sandstone
for distant city buildings. We work
between walls they made possible.

Silence cradles the lake,
invites us to listen.

Apostle Fall

Kenneth Pobo

The calendar, a hooting owl,
a sound that fades quickly.

The Lake barely holds
onto summer, sees it slip away.
A single snowflake
blots fall out. Over:

the ferry from Bayfield
to Madeline Island,
stand-up comedian captains.
Wind slaps housefronts
overlooking the bay.

A piping plover, now flown
to the Gulf of Mexico,
kicks sand far away. Late

autumn yearns for a song
it will never hear again.

THE BIG SING

Mary Riley

We drove along U.S. Route 41 at dusk,
stands of jack pine thick with red-eyed deer,
on our way to listen to the men sing.
It was the end of a warm spring day in May,
but for many of the men, my father among them,
the year was well into November.

These grandfathers, fathers and sons, uncles and nephews
left their offices, stations, workshops, factory floors,
laboratories, classrooms, easy chairs, corner taverns,
and all manner of title and occupation
to simply sing as a band of brothers.

The men's choruses assembled one by one
in the town on the edge of Lake Superior;
they hailed from Milwaukee, Negaunee, and Ishpeming,
Marquette, Gwinn, Rhinelander and Munising.
Older and younger men together cast long shadows
as they strolled through the parking lot and filed through
the entrance of the public high school auditorium.

My father looked strong and vivacious in his tuxedo.
The last time he wore *any* tuxedo was at my wedding.
And before that, his own.

Then the auditorium lights dimmed,
piano strains quieted the crowd and
the men, multi-voiced, sang with one accord:
baritones weaving through lush groves of voice,
tenors leaping above into color and light,
basses sounding undercurrents of approaching night.

The men sang spirited numbers belonging
to a simpler time: radio tunes, Broadway tunes,
gospel songs, patriotic songs, the old standbys.
All of which belonged entirely to them as they sang.
The harsh stagelight showed weathered faces,
many men bald or balding, some wearing rings, or without.
But all with clear and shining eyes staring out into the dark.

They sang to the full, these otherwise silent oaks at dawn.
And yet, after the concert was over and the afterglow
party began, I thought I heard their songs escape through
the entranceway and roam into the infinite black.
Songs speaking to men in forgotten graves at the bottom
of the treacherous Lake, songs speaking to ghosts of men
wandering rocky shorelines and ruins of abandoned mining
towns.

And I think of how one day,
once I too have crossed over,
I will reach across the starlit night
to clasp my father's hand and ask him
to sing one more song,
a welcoming lullaby perhaps,
the way the men sang their entire lives that night.

YOOPER ROCKHOUNDS

Mary Riley

Frequently spotted in Marquette County,
this crazy species of person hunts for rocks
as though seeking out old friends:

agates, those smooth-talkers
with their colorful stories, they'll glide
into your jeans pocket in no time;

specular hematites, the flashy and glamorous ones;
sandstones, always unassuming and delicate;
staurolites, so gregarious and devout.

And those eccentrics, oolitic jasper and jaspelite,
with whom you'd share a bottle of red and laugh all night,
recounting striped hijinks under a micaceous moon.

Then there are granites of Pre-Cambrian ancestry,
of great stoic cliffs jutting out of this Great Inland Sea.
These are the elders, the survivors, the guides.
Time and wisdom rest compactly in the palm of your hand.

They'll listen to your dreams, your despairs,
and faithfully hold your secrets, your tellings.
Long after you've paddled through in this canoe.
Long after this day fades away into twilight, then night.

LAKE SUPERIOR POEM #3

George Roberts

And then, after walking, find yourself at the edge
of this inland ocean. Your eyes continue out
even as your feet pause. Instead of cascading waves,
the booming voice of the surf, there is only silence,
steelblue water, and a solitary loon, its black head
and sinuate neck perfectly reflected
in the still, glassy water.

Do they not mate for life? What does a single loon
in Lake Superior mean? That we were given this thirst
for love in the womb, when we too drifted in dark water?

WELDER

Mary Kay Rummel

From the freighter's side an explosion
star fall meeting of torch and hull
like those white fireworks against
a winter carnival sky, in the dark,
ice sculptures. I watch from a window
thinking of the welder at work in that wind.

Behind the boat the bridge bucks and rises.
Trucks and cars roll over its arched center
like necklace or rosary beads, a cold mathematics,
reminding me of my statistics teacher

who filled the board with formulas as he
talked nonstop—I thought he spoke
a different language like a poem in Irish.
When I listened I heard patterns I could recognize.

Now as I go round the mysteries of fears and losses
the sicknesses, the good byes, the letting go
I am looking for patterns in ice, in fire,
patterns spinning from planet to eye.

The welder will finish, the air will turn
bread colored, and the freighter will sail
from this harbor toward Sault Sainte Marie.

Until then we live in a blur of blue and white—
more light, snowing.

FISHING

Yvonne Rutford

"I have to focus on the work I have to do, and on the beauty around me. Yes, lift the net up over the bow. And there, the flash of silver herring below in the clear, cold water."
—Stephen Dahl, *Knife Island: Circling a Year in a Herring Skiff*

On the commute where the road makes a sweeping turn toward town and Lake Superior spreads out before the motorists, the water is the color of mercury and ribbed with waves. One-footers? Two? It's hard to tell a half mile from shore in a sixty-mile-an-hour glance. What kind of sea would Stephen call this? The sun bores through a cleft in the clouds and lays a streak of gold across the water. I think of him out there, his stiff fingers plying the icy nets. Alone and in the world in a way I long for. After reading how he circled the year in a skiff, I wanted to change my life and swore the least I would do is commute along the scenic route and stand on the shore of that great lake every day, breathe its icy breath and feel its cold spray. But late for work, here I am on the expressway again, only glimpsing that vast, unrelenting wilderness. The radio clock reads nine, and I know I should tune into the outrage of *Amy Goodman and Democracy Now: the War and Peace Report*, because as the bumper stickers say, if I'm not outraged I'm not paying attention, but this morning I am paying attention. To the lake, where miles from shore a fisherman hopes to draw upward some bright flash, breaking the surface of darkness, and so do I.

MORNING

Ellie Schoenfeld

Peninsula licks water,
light splinters bounce while
I am concentrating
on the slow wave
of breath,
inhaling while a government
on the other side
of the planet changes,
exhaling while ours does not.
But just for today
I will not dwell on that.
I will go to the Lake
for a baptism.
I will remember
that I am mostly water,
will return to the source
and give thanks,
emerge cold and purified
with the music of
fish and seaweed.
A distant ocean beat
in this water that I could follow
to the Nile, the Congo, the Amazon

where a thousand other women
are standing
toes splayed in the silt
drinking in the stories
of the earth.
Healing and regenerating
in the dance
of waving and breathing
waving and breathing
waving and breathing
and breathing.

An Unrefined Northern Metaphor

Ellie Schoenfeld

There is nothing refined
about the way the water
meets the shore—
all that pounding and lapping
and the leaving of broken glass,
driftwood, a rusty can.
No pearls here, no shells to hold
to your ear to hear secrets.
If you are holding bread
to cast onto the waters
the seagulls will swoop in
to divert that good intention
to a more primal impulse,
a primal hunger.
Everything here is hungry.
This is not an
elegant well-behaved place.
This water will break
your boat in two,
will suck the living warmth
out of your body in minutes

and throw your broken bones
back to the shore
where a vulture,
who has never learned table manners,
is waiting to eat.

Mining Country

on Michigan's Upper Peninsula, circa 1975

Steven Sher

Beyond Negaunee when the wind
comes off the lake, it lifts
the ore plant's plume straight for
these woods: each tree, a pink-
dipped crayon stacked on end;
the roads, pink strokes; each rock,
a splotch of splattered paint;
the sky, a limpid pink.
The miners' lives become tight
fists nothing can pry apart.
Not far from the last abandoned
heap of slag, their homes
wear bright pink coats of dust:
wood slats to shingles, window frames—
pink frost across the plastic sheets
or caked on glass—to the back porch.
Distilled pink liquid trickles out
the drainpipe now. That burning
furnace, active mind, consumes
the unexpected hope: pink flowers
briefly blooming here, their beds
banked high behind the kitchen.

And when, next bloodletting
of earth, it rains, the pasty pink
runoff will pool into pink pits:
a stagnant glop, once showers stop,
scumming these puddles pink.

SOME DISTANCE OFFSHORE

Phillip Sterling

Halfway across Lake Superior
the Ranger III is a shadow-puppet
projected on a screen: horn,
at intervals, the only evidence
of time passing, distance,

until the fog lifts
and curious passengers
turn from their friendly gambling
to grumble at the rail: *Nothing,*
one says, *as far as the eye can see.*

If nothing, I think (kindly),
you must need glasses, for there
is clear demarcation for me: the sky
three shades of silver
lighter than Superior, itself

the pewter gray of lake trout—horizon,
then, as far as a person can see—
and beyond the horizon:
tomorrow,
and the arms of someone who loves us

welcoming us home. "Nothing,
at bottom," I want to say (unkindly),
quoting Philip Booth,
"is to have nothing at heart."
Yet I keep the thought to myself.

It's nothing if not obvious—
the gray / silver stretching forward
and back, as in a stubborn
present tense of fog—the obvious
that's better left unspoken.

LAKE SUPERIOR BEACHCOMBING

Amy Jo Swing

I

The dog and I walk down
to see what the water has
churned up—some birch bark,
plastic, bony sticks—
our feet spread the water
from the sand or make sink holes
between the rocks.

Some days we really *look*
for things: pick up bits
of glass, finger the edges,
throw them back
if they're not worn enough.

Today, I see breasts
in the waves maybe.
Fallen trees break
the low wind. Smooth as they are,
all the rocks just lie there.

II

Just when I think I've got the water
figured out, it pushes all
the rocks up on shore—
fifteen feet at least—bringing
the cartilage of an animal skull
which the dog pees on. Once
expectation breaks, anything's
fair game, even the red,
plastic ribbon on the sand,
the bicycle seat, carburetor,
even the seagulls
staggering in the wind, the waves
hitting the pier at an angle,
sending spray up
one plank at a time.

III

The beach is giving up a regular
harvest today—leaves, straw, red
berries, even apples and pinecones.
I have to hold my hand over my ears
to hear the waves above the wind.
It only takes one wet, rainy day
to take all the leaves off the branches:
harvest to husk. The waves change color
four or five times before they meet

the shore: gray, green, brown, white, spray.
The clouds are moving Southeast,
a Canadian wind herding them.
It's twenty-two degrees
in mid-October. This is how
weather is supposed to be.
Biting. Bitten.

IV

Lots of bricks on the shore today,
bricks and glass—as if the lake were trying
to build a house. There's metal too—
pieces twisted into the shapes of waves,
or pieces pounded thin like *milagros*, promises—
and, as always, the stones.

LAKE SUPERIOR—A LOVE SONG FROM THE LAKE

Sara Thomsen

Wood fire flickers, shadows on the wall
And the nightfall pulls her blanket upon us all

Bone bare branches against the sky
Solitude smiles at the snow driftin' by
Ice cold waves wash hard upon the shore
And the wild wind knockin' at your door

And the water will whisper a love song in your ear
"Come near. I will always be here."

Bird song beckons on the air
Buds on the branches open like a prayer
The crashing of the waves carves your name upon the shore
"Evermore! It is you I adore."

And the water will whisper a love song in your ear
"Come near. I will always be here."

Flowers white, yellow, pink and blue
Berries and black bear, eagle flying true
Lady's slipper, loon song, stories in the stone
Coming home. You will never be alone

For the water will whisper a love song in your ear
"Come near. I will always be here."

Grass turns to yellow, the ferns are brown
Chill in the air, frost on the ground
Fire fill the leaves, and they fall on the forest floor
Breezes blow, and bring them to the shore

Where the water will whisper, a love song in your ear
"Come near. I will always be here."

Wood fire flickers, shadows on the wall
And the nightfall pulls her blanket upon us all

A Random Gust from the North

Connie Wanek

Run-off

Another hottest summer ever.
Storms with the violence of a broken atom.
Storms that drove the boats in
and smashed them in their slips. Power out for days,
so we lived by the sky, like any animal.
Run-off turned the bay red
as from some ancient slaughter—
the smelt runs, perhaps, every spring of your youth
when fish crowded the river mouths
so thickly you could reach down with only your hands
and take all you wanted
and people did. In the evening
we knelt on the boulders by the big lake
and washed our forearms
in the surges that rose against the stone,
and the water we loved was cold enough to kill us.

Sunfish

His ribs were thick as barrel staves,
his heart full of chambers such as waves
carve out of granite,
smooth caverns accessible only by boat.

His toes were like mushrooms,
misshapen by the sealed can of a boot
and yellowed, homely,
each with a thick indelicate scale.
They had the look of fish bait
as indeed they were
when as a child he sat on the weathered dock,
the soft gray boards, his feet
dangling in the lake, and sunfish
nibbled his toes. Sunnies.
What was death, but sunlight on the water?
Now he set herring nets on summer mornings
while the village slept. His boat was simple,
plain, a work boat among the pleasure craft
in the marina. Nothing polished,
no illusions, no vanity.
He left the harbor on an open palm
held out to the lake and sky.
He was an offering.
Good days he filled the boat with thrashing fish
drowning in oxygen. It was the same fish
over and over, like page after page
to the illiterate.
This man with a kind disposition
sold his catch, and thus he lived.
"North," he said, and it seemed the word itself
spoke, offering hardship and darkness and solitude,
and he trembled like a compass needle.

South Wind

Sometimes he caught a fish that had cancer.
A south wind carried the stench of the paper mill.
South. A single city sixty miles across.
Thousands of cars on the freeway,
all sizes and sorts, like fish
forced together by low water
or by a net. The air he was obliged to breathe,
air that had passed through
smokestacks and motors and ducts and countless
living lungs before his and after,
air that had a history,
that had come to the city years ago
blown in from the alfalfa fields
to enter a copse of mirrored towers
now seen, now lost in the sky,
to swirl in a courtyard
rising and falling through the hours
without passion or purpose
but with exhilarating ease.
Flocks of ravens gathered in the dirty park,
shining like the ugly jewelry of the Aztecs
polished by slaves.
Heat waves rose from the grid, a conflagration
that seared the silver bellies of the jets.
There were highways among the clouds
or else the sky was but another blue sea
and planes were passenger ships,
as birds were fish,
as wind was a current.

Why lament? So goes the wind. South.
Here is the puncture
where poison entered the body.

A Small Vessel in the Swells
He took up the rope
and drew the boat toward him like a pony.
It woke as he stepped into it
and settled obediently under his weight.
Then the canter of a small vessel in the swells,
the bow high, power
from the churning hindquarters.
He went out against the will of the lake.
No horizon, the water red as the sunrise:
he was crossing the sky.
Later it would be rough,
perhaps dangerous,
the warning repeated every few seconds
until it goes unheeded.
Where does a wave begin?
Before memory,
in the quick pulse of a mother's blood
pouring into the bay of the womb.
Impossible to say whether the water
speaks from within or without.
Ashore again, he felt the earth
rock on its fulcrum; standing on shore
he felt land-sick, drained, short of breath.

The North Shore

A cabin so small it is like a woodpecker hole
smelling of fresh pine pitch.
Like a new-made pauper's coffin.
Calm today. One feels the depth of the lake,
the weight of an iron anchor
falling through the fathoms.
Here or there a surface disturbance,
a boat wake, a few gulls bickering over fish offal,
then a random gust from the north.
The lake wrinkles the way a horse,
dozing in the shade, jerks its skin
where a fly lands.
Waves come to shore backwards, blindly,
like a horse backing into wagon traces
with a sack over its head.
If a horse knew its strength
it could never be tamed.

A Last Reading

The north pole. Instruments alone confirm it.
And what if the instruments disagree?
Can there be such an absolute arrival?
Or does realization come later,
far too late for the champagne.
And what of ambition?
Surely it precedes a man by months, years,
and has already published its memoirs.
Here one senses the attention
of every compass in the world

pointing like a crowd of fingers
toward a tightrope stretched between
clouds. A lone figure looks everywhere
but down. So much light,
light to spare, light to spread on the ice like salt.
The pole afloat; we are neither first
nor last, though perhaps nearer the last.
We need no instruments.
The equatorial vertigo subsides;
the heat of exertion dissipates.
We have no fear of falling.
We can never be lost.

CARTOGRAPHY

Laurelyn Whitt

"If one no longer has land
but has the memory of land,
then one can make a map."
—*Anne Michaels*

once there were no borders

only the blue,
the white, the
wind
the huge indifference
of Superior

great girth lapping at
granite, pine
    to the south, the long
buttressing reach of a
peninsula

*

the hand of the cartographer
opened and closed
on this immense presence

the futility of the
gesture   massive:

no border so thin or
inconsequential as the
ram-straight line
severing Superior   its waters

currents,   like the slow ripples
of geese overhead,   flowing
unimpeded

*

more malleable, the land
as a medium
for borders,   more
receptive to the
    cleaving art

releasing the lower
peninsula of the lake
from the grip of a
continent

but here, the cartographer's
dividing hand has
unintended effects

freeing the shape of an
eagle, head lowered
soaring

and below,
the vastness of
Superior
      held silent,
      captive
      in her gaze

MÉTIS

Laurelyn Whitt

"I learned the hard way that one who swims
between cultures can get stranded, cut off
from either shore."
—*Christine Welsh*

All day spent
drifting on a
liquid borderline

wondering which
country & when,
disoriented.

Too far out on
Superior for this

the fragility
of the canoe
manifest:

ocher skin
thin, translucent

meant to skim lightly,
    the brush of
    air on water.

Too slim a vessel
for plying such
uncertain surfaces.

*

A whole life spent
gliding through
a borderworld;

it wells up,
at the edges
   of others.

Across the lake
gone glassy & flat,
a long, piercing wail:

a loon dives before me,
slipping easily
   between elements.

Several small ripples
then nothing
   a fluency
so complete it swells the

heart with awe,
envy.

To know it once
would console
   a lifetime.

MAKING THE LAKE MY NORTH

Morgan Grayce Willow

As cardinals give the sun direction
and lupine flare their posts,
I reorient my intentions.
In the act of listening,
stories, like dew, settle.
Birch bark talks.
An eagle feather falls.
The lake, flat, deceives its depth.
My only conversation, the weather.

Does changing places, then, remake us?
Some weeds travel with me:
the bluestem, the cattail, milkweed.
They're seeds in my hair.
Some trees I must visit
on pages or in earth.
A shift in the field shifts me.
Molecules align with magnetic force.

If molecules align with force,
then a shift in the field shifts me,
whether on pages or in the earth.
There are trees I must visit.

There are seeds in my hair
of bluestem, cattail, and milkweed.
These weeds travel with me,
despite the change place makes in us.

My conversation is with the weather,
with the lake, flat, deceptive, deep.
An eagle feather falls.
Birch bark talks
stories. Dew settles
in the act of listening.
I reorient my intentions
to lupine, flaring their posts,
to cardinals, to the sun's direction.
I'm making the lake my north.

NIGHT SWIM IN LAKE SUPERIOR

Patricia Zontelli

I go for a night swim
in the dusk hour: so this
is what it's like to live.
I dip, spurt like a dolphin,
heart beating madly
as a muskrat paddles out—
taking the night air
in his city, twirling his mustache.
Evening brings
the slow dark, the panting but
hushed self, elderberry bush
mere shadow. Dog Star,
up there as usual, eyes
us below like so many bones,
protectively. All treachery eased.
Here I am, not in water but,
at this late warm hour, still sitting
on the grassy bank. Maybe it's true,
I can grow old gracefully. Tonight,
I look into the dark with no regret.
I'm happy here, in this body,
these bones, uncomplicated
by glare, heat of sunlight.

Notes on Contributors

Angela Ahlgren is a writer and scholar teaching in the Department of Performance Studies at Texas A & M University. She was born in Cloquet, Minnesota, and has lived in Michigan, Ohio, and Texas. She enjoys spending summers with family and friends in beautiful Duluth.

James Armstrong has published poems in *Split Rock Review, Terrain, Gulf Coast, Orion, Poetry East* and elsewhere. He is the author of *Monument in a Summer Hat* (New Issues Press, 1999) and *Blue Lash* (Milkweed Editions, 2006). He is Professor of English at Winona State University in Winona, Minnesota.

Milton J. Bates is a retired English professor who lives on Lake Superior near Marquette, Michigan. He has published several non-fiction books, including, most recently, *The Bark River Chronicles: Stories from a Wisconsin Watershed* (2012). His poems have appeared in various magazines and anthologies.

Samuel Black arrived on Lake Superior's North Shore in August, 1995. Since then, he has taught writing at local colleges, directed musical groups, played organs or pianos, and written music and drama reviews. His website, *www.samuelcblack.com*, tries to stay current with his schedule.

Kimberly Blaeser is the author of three poetry collections—*Apprenticed to Justice, Absentee Indians and Other Poems,* and *Trailing You.* She is the current Wisconsin Poet Laureate. A Professor at University of Wisconsin—Milwaukee, Blaeser teaches Creative Writing, Native American Literature, and American Nature Writing. Her poetry, short fiction, and essays have been widely anthologized, most recently in *The Heath Anthology of American Literature,* and selections of her poetry have been translated into several languages including Spanish, Norwegian, Indonesian, and French.

Gary Boelhower's recent books include *Marrow, Muscle, Flight: Poems,* published by Wildwood River Press (2011) and winner of the Midwest Book Award, *Choose Wisely: Practical Insights from Spiritual Traditions,* published by Paulist Press (2013), and *Mountain 10: Climbing the Labyrinth Within,* published by Mountain Ten Resources (2013).

Jeffrey D. Boldt, a Wisconsin administrative law judge, has published numerous poems, short stories and essays. Publication credits include: *Berkeley Poetry Review, The MacGuffin, Blueline, The Wallace Stevens Journal, Interim, Clare, Great River Review, Mickle Street Review, The Missing Slate, Seems, The J Journal, Tikkun* and *Agave.* His website is Jeffrey Boldt Writes.

Dan Campion is the author of *Peter De Vries and Surrealism* and a co-editor of *Walt Whitman: The Measure of His Song.* His poems have appeared in the anthology *The Heart of All That Is: Reflections on Home* and in many magazines, including *Blue Unicorn, Ekphrasis, Light, Measure,* and *Poetry.*

Taina Maki Chahal is a writer and educator whose latest writing "At the Bottom of Amethyst," co-written with sister Della Bitove, was staged at the 10x10 Play Showcase. With sister Katja Maki, she staged "Minna Canth: There's No Stopping Her." She reads her poems at the Northern Woman's Bookstore and with Random Acts of Poetry.

Sharon Chmielarz's latest book is *Visibility: Ten Miles, a Prairie Memoir in Photography and Poetry* (2015). Some of her grief poems are in *18 Minnesota Poets* (2015). For other work, please visit *www.sharonchmielarz.com.*

David R. Clowers' poems have appeared in *Your Daily Poem, Re-Verse, Fox Cry, Verse Wisconsin, Peninsula Pulse, Knock,* and the Wisconsin Fellowship of Poets calendars. His poems also received recognition from WFOP's Triad and the Grutzmacher Poetry Expose contests. A chapbook, *Shedding My Three Piece Birthday Suit* was published in 2010.

Carolyn Colburn writes fiction, creative nonfiction and poetry. She received an MFA in Writing from Goddard College and has been awarded a Minnesota State Arts Board grant and a Loft-McKnight Fellowship. Her novel, *Minimum Maintenance,* was published in 2010. Her work can be found at *sixspruce.blogspot.com.*

Deborah Cooper is the author of five volumes of poetry and has had her work published in numerous journals and anthologies. She facilitates poetry groups at the St. Louis County Jail and was the 2012-2014 Duluth Poet Laureate.

Florence Chard Dacey has published several poetry collections, including *Rock Worn by Water,* poems about our place within the natural world. Recently relocated to Florida, she lived for forty-three years in Cottonwood, Minnesota. Her website is *florencedacey.com.*

Norita Dittberner-Jax lives in Saint Paul. Her poem "Superior at the Shoreline: February" was written after taking her grandsons, Gabe and Zeli Zaun, to the lake to witness its icy splendor. Her books of poems include *Stopping for Breath* (Nodin Press), *The Watch* (Whistling Shade Press), *Longing for Home* (Pudding House Press), and *What They Always Were* (New Rivers Press).

Deborah H. Doolittle lives and works in Jacksonville, North Carolina. Other recent work may be seen in *Barbaric Yawp, Nerve Cowboy, Plainsongs, Poem, Poet's Expresso Review, Ship of Fools,* and *Trajectory.*

Barbara Draper is a longtime Michigander who recently moved to Minneapolis. For a good time, she enjoys friends, movies, downhill skiing and playing with her two granddaughters. Her poems have appeared or soon will be published in *Grey Sparrow, Passagers, Split Rock Review,* and *The Aurorean.*

Heid E. Erdrich is author of four poetry collections, most recently *Cell Traffic: New and Selected Poems.* Her first non-fiction work, *Original Local: Indigenous Foods, Stories and Recipes,* was published in 2013. She directs Wiigwaas Press, which publishes Ojibwe language books and she teaches in the Low-Residency MFA at Augsburg College. Heid is Ojibwe and enrolled at Turtle Mountain.

Michelle Bonczek Evory is the author of *The Art of the Nipple* (Orange Monkey, 2013) and the forthcoming Open SUNY Textbook *Naming the Unnameable: An Approach to Poetry for New Generations*. Her poetry is featured in the 2013 Best New Poets Anthology. She mentors poets at The Poet's Billow, *thepoetsbillow.com*.

Teresa Boyle Falsani, a Maine native, has lived in Duluth, Minnesota since 1973, and still wishes Lake Superior smelled like salt. A mother of two, she worked in advertising and taught English literature. Her writing appears in several anthologies and journals and on her blog at *tbfalsani@wordpress.com*.

Lynda Ferguson was raised in the Badlands of the Dakotas, and has lived in the Arrowhead region for just as long. She is the owner of Road Kill Theater and Design, and is currently working on an arts-based curriculum for a children's educational television program.

Phil Fitzpatrick is a retired English teacher who first paddled the Boundary Waters in 1958. As a canoe guide at a private youth camp on the Gunflint Trail, he familarized himself with voyageur lore and paddled many of their fur trade routes. "Voyageur" is his second anthologized poem.

Margot Fortunato Galt is the author of 5 books of nonfiction, notably with George Morrison, *Turning the Feather Around* (1998) and *Up to the Plate: The All-American Girls Professional Baseball League* (1995)—both finalists for the Minnesota Book Award. Her poetry is collected in *Between the Houses* (2004).

Julie Gard's prose poetry collection, *Home Studies,* is forthcoming from New Rivers Press in Fall, 2015. Chapbooks include *Obscura: The Daguerreotype Series* (Finishing Line Press) and *Russia in 17 Objects* (Tiger's Eye Press). She is Assistant Professor of Writing at the University of Wisconsin-Superior and can be found online at *www.juliegard.com.*

Jane Graham George is the author of two books of poetry, both published by Red Dragonfly Press. Her poems have appeared in *Poetry Australia, Spirit Horse, The Aurorean,* and *County Lines.* She has lived in California, Minnesota and most currently in New Zealand, where she works as a librarian and lives on the Kapiti Coast near Wellington.

Candace Ginsberg's life has been shaped by Lake Superior—from rafts built of log-boom pulp logs as a child, to rock collections, reveling in big waves during Nor'easters, bird-watching, sun and moon rises, and a lifetime of sailing its calms and gales.

Linda Glaser feels very fortunate to live so near Lake Superior that she sees it every day and can sometimes actually walk on it. This poem emerged from one such experience on a stunningly cold and beautiful day. She also writes children's books. You can visit her at *www.LindaGlaserAuthor.com.*

Tom Hansen is a retired teacher living in the Black Hills of South Dakota. His poems have appeared in *The Literary Review, The Midwest Quarterly, Poetry Northwest, Weber: The Contemporary West,* and others. His book, *Falling to Earth,* was published by BOA Editions in 2006.

Gwen Hart teaches writing at Buena Vista University. Her stories and poems have appeared in literary journals and anthologies such as *Lake Effect, Calliope, Stories from Where We Live: The Great Lakes,* and *PRISM International.* Her poetry collection, *Lost and Found,* is available from David Robert Books.

Mara Hart has been an editor of three periodicals and three anthologies. A former librarian and teacher, she now is a writer, mentor and editor. She lives in Duluth, Minnesota with two cats and many books.

Susan Carol Hauser is a poet, essayist, and natural history writer. Her books include *Wild Sugar: The Pleasures of Making Maple Syrup.* Her awards include a McKnight Artist Fellowship-Loft Award for Poetry and two Minnesota State Arts Board Artist Initiative Grants in Nonfiction. Her website is *www.susancarol-hauser.com.*

Susan Hawkinson co-authored *Timber Connections: The Joyce Lumber Story,* a 2003 Minnesota Book Award finalist. Her illustrated book, *Tina Christina Sestina,* written for children and adults, was published in 2013. Currently she is writing a play for children set in the BWCAW as well as double-voiced poems with Loree Miltich.

Eva Hooker is Professor of English and Writer in Residence at Saint Mary's College, Notre Dame, Indiana. *The Winter Keeper,* a hand bound chapbook (Chapiteau Press, Montpelier, Vermont, 2000), was a finalist for the Minnesota Book Award in Poetry in 2001. Her poems have recently appeared in *The New England*

Review, Agni, The Harvard Review, et al. Lake Superior and Madeline Island have left their profound watermark on the poems that make up *Notes for Survival in the Wilderness* (Chapiteau Press, 2013). *Godwit* (3 Taos Press) is forthcoming.

Ann Iverson is the author of three poetry collections: *Come Now to the Window* (Laurel Poetry Collective, 2003); *Definite Space* (Holy Cow! Press, 2007); and *Art Lessons* (Holy Cow! Press, 2011). Her poetry has appeared on The Writer's Almanac and the MPR blog. She is also a visual artist and her work has one permanent installation at the University of Minnesota Amplatz Hospital. She is a graduate of both the MFA and MALS programs at Hamline University.

Janet Jerve's poems have appeared in many literary journals, including *Poetry East* and *Water-Stone Review,* and in two anthologies published by Holy Cow! Press, *Beloved on the Earth* and *The Heart of All That Is.* Her first poetry book, *Excavation,* was published by North Star Press (2013).

Jim Johnson has published seven books of poetry. His most recent, *The First Day Of Spring In Northern Minnesota* (Red Dragonfly Press) was a Minnesota Book Award Finalist. He is the 2014-2016 Poet Laureate of Duluth, Minnesota.

Meridel Kahl retired in 2013 after 45 years of teaching—the last twenty-seven years were at the College of Saint Scholastica in Duluth, Minnesota. She loves every minute of her new life, especially the time she has to write.

Maggie Kazel is a writer, mom, and former radio producer. Her writings appear in the Wildwood River Press's *Migrations* anthology, *Thunderbird Review, Evergreen Chronicle, Sibling Rivalry Press,* and other regional and national journals. She works for Rural AIDS Action Network, and believes in Grace Paley's view: "Life is too short, and Art too long."

Susan Deborah King has taught creative writing and led retreats on creativity and spirituality in Minneapolis and Maine. She is the author of five full-length poetry collections including *One Breasted-Woman* and *Dropping into the Flower* from Holy Cow! Press. She lives with her husband near Portland, Maine.

Mary F. Lee lives four miles from mercurial Lake Superior. Her poems have appeared in *Dust & Fire, Minnetonka Review, POETRY Humor Issue, Black Fox Literary Magazine, Noteworthy: A Collaborative Performance by Poets & Musicians* (Duluth, MN), and *Aqueous Magazine.* She was selected for Ted Kooser's UMD advanced writing workshop in 2008. She is a professional saxophonist.

Cecilia Lieder is a woodcut artist, poet, small press publisher and gallery owner who has lived on the shore of Lake Superior most of her life. Rarely out of sight from it, the Lake has been her mentor, refuge, nemesis, and muse—a central magnetic force shaping her journey. Please visit her website, *www.cecilialieder.com*

Judy Lindberg grew up in West Duluth and taught at Penn State University. She has been published in many journals and anthologies. She and her family own a small cabin north of Duluth where she spends most of her time with loons and walleyes.

Micky McGilligan has work in such journals as *Loonfeather* and *Main Channel Voices,* and in anthologies published by Poetry Harbor, Savage Press and others. She has been active in the writing community for 40 years through organizations like North Shore Poets in Two Harbors and Lake Superior Writers in Duluth, Minnesota.

Lisa McKhann lives, writes, works, dances, and directs the non-profit Project Lulu in Duluth where she has lived for the past 18 years with her husband Pete.

Pamela Mittlefehldt is a poet, editor, writer, and fiddler. The focus of her work is on the power of story to transform our lives as individuals and as communities. She is currently working on a cross-genre project on food, justice, place, and spirit.

Yvonne Pearson's poetry has appeared in many publications, including *Main Street Rag, Wolf Head Quarterly, Open to Interpretation, Chrysalis,* and others. She received a Loft Creative Non-fiction Award, a Minnesota State Arts Board Grant, and the Shabo Award in Children's Literature. Her picture book is forthcoming from the Minnesota Historical Society Press.

Susan Perala-Dewey lives in Duluth and teaches at the University of Minnesota-Duluth. During her half century on planet Earth, she has spent 90% of her days within a mile of Lake Superior. She can't imagine living away from this holy body of water.

Kenneth Pobo has a new book, *Bend of Quiet,* forthcoming from Blue Lights Press. His work appears in the Holy Cow! Press anthology *The Heart of All That Is: Reflections on Home* (2013).

Mary Riley was born in Milwaukee, Wisconsin. A graduate of Beloit College, she has vivid memories of the heart-stopping beauty of Lake Superior, and of time spent in Marquette, Michigan and other lakeshore towns in the Upper Penisula. She lives, works, and writes poetry in Chicago, Illinois.

George Roberts continues to live in North Minneapolis, continues to write poetry every day, continues to be surprised by what the moon does to the night sky.

Mary Kay Rummel's seventh book of poetry, *The Lifeline Trembles*, was published as a winner of the 2014 Blue Light Book Award. Recent publications include poems in *Nimrod*, *Pirene's Fountain*, and *New Poetry from the Midwest*. Retired from the University of Minnesota, Duluth, she teaches at California State University, Channel Islands, commuting between the two states.

Yvonne Rutford is among the five generations of her family who have lived along, and loved, the shores of Lake Superior. From her home on one of the Lake's tributary streams, she is inspired by and writes about the landscape of northeastern Minnesota. She teaches writing at the University of Wisconsin-Superior.

Ellie Schoenfeld practices poetry in Duluth, MN. She has one collection in print, *The Dark Honey: New and Used Poems* (Clover Valley Press, 2009), and has poetry in *Bound Together Like the Grasses* (Clover Valley Press, 2013), an anthology with four other members of her writing group. She also enjoys collaborating with musicians and with artists from other genres.

Steven Sher lived in Marquette, Michigan in the mid-1970s (as an editor for *People & Places* magazine). His 14 books include two new poetry collections, *The House of Washing Hands* (Pecan Grove Press) and *Grazing on Stars: Collected Poems* (Presa Press). *Bending with the Wind* (Cross-Cultural Communications) is forthcoming. He now lives in Jerusalem (Israel).

Phillip Sterling's most recent book is *In Which Brief Stories Are Told* (short fiction, Wayne State University Press). He is also the author of the poetry collection *Mutual Shores* and three chapbook-length series of poems (*Significant Others, Quatrains,* and *Abeyance*). In August, 2014, he served as Artist-in-Residence for Isle Royale National Park.

Amy Jo Swing has lived in Alaska, Indiana, and Texas and ultimately chose the shores of Lake Superior for her home. She spends her days teaching writing, skiing, hiking, and playing near the lake, and trying to keep up with her wife, two daughters, and schnoodle puppy.

Sara Thomsen, a singer-songwriter from the Twin Ports of Duluth-Superior, has been dubbed by listeners as the "Mary Oliver of Song." A recipient of numerous songwriting awards, Thomsen's recordings include *Somewhere to Begin, Winter Wanderings, Three Altos: One Voice, Everything Changes, Three Altos: Camaradas, By Breath, Fertile Ground* and *Arise.* Her website is *www.sarathomsen. com.*

Connie Wanek is the author of three poetry books and a volume of short prose. Her forthcoming book: *Rival Gardens: New and Selected Poems,* will appear in late 2015 from the University of Nebraska Press.

Laurelyn Whitt's poems have appeared in various, primarily North American, journals including *Nimrod International, Tampa Review, Puerto Del Sol, Malahat Review, PRISM International, Rattle,* and *Descant.* The author of four award-winning poetry collections, her most recent book, *Tether* (Seraphim Editions) won the 2013 Lansdowne Prize. She lives in Minnedosa, Manitoba.

Morgan Grayce Willow has published three poetry collections, most recently *Dodge & Scramble.* Other poetry titles include *Between, Silk, The Maps are Words,* and *Arpeggio of Appetite.* She has received awards from the Minnesota State Arts Board, McKnight Foundation, and Witter Bynner Foundation. She lives in Minneapolis and teaches at the Loft.

Patricia Zontelli's first and second poetry collections were published by New Rivers Press; the latter, *Red Cross Dog,* was a finalist for the National Poetry Series. Her poems have appeared in *Beloit Poetry Journal, Connecticut Poetry Review, Georgetown Review, Gettysburg Review, Slant, Water~Stone Review* and a number of other journals and anthologies.

Permissions and Sources

We wish to express our thanks to authors, editors and publishers and other copyright holders for their permission to include the works indicated below.

"Oligotrophic," by James Armstrong is reprinted from *Blue Lash* by James Armstrong (Milkweed Editions, 2005) by permission of the author.

"Windbound with Dostoevsky," by Milton J. Bates first appeared in the Winter 2014 issue of *Great Lakes Review,* and is reprinted by permission of the author.

"Counterpoint," by Samuel Black is reprinted from *Out of Words* (Volume 8, 2003-04), a College of Saint Scholastica literary journal, by permission of the author.

"Slippage," and "Eloquence of Earth," by Kimberly Blaeser, were published in an earlier form in *Mujeres Talk* (May, 2014) and are reprinted by permission of the author.

"After Sailing," by Gary Boelhower, was previously published in *Marrow, Muscle, Flight: Poems* published by Wildwood River Press (2011); "Dance at Dawn," by Gary Boelhower, previously appreared in *Freshwater Review* (Spring, 2014) and reprinted by permission of the author.

"The North (After Borges)," by Jeffrey D. Boldt, first appeared in *The MacGuffin* (Volume VII, #1, 1990) and is reprinted by permission of the author.

"After All of My Life," by Florence Dacey, appeared in an earlier version in *Rock Worn by Water* and online at womensvoicesfor-change.org, and is reprinted by permission of the author.

"Superior at the Shoreline: February," by Norita Dittberner-Jax, appears in *Stopping for Breath* (Nodin Press, 2014); "Levitating Toward Duluth," by Norita Dittberner-Jax, was published in *What They Always Wore* (New Rivers Press, 1995) and is reprinted by permission of the author.

"Water Colors," by Deborah H. Doolittle, previously appeared in *Colorado Crossing* and is reprinted by permission of the author.

"Gitche Onagaaming," by Heid E. Erdrich was originally published in *National Monuments* (Michigan State University Press, 2008) and is reprinted by permission of the author.

"Wooded Road, Lake Superior," by Michelle Bonczek Evory, is reprinted from Connotations Press, by permission of the author.

"Lake Drought" by Margot Fortunato Galt, was previously published in *The Quiet Eye: Thirteen Ways of Looking at Nature* (2009) and is reprinted by permission of the author.

"Crossing Over," by Candace Ginsberg, was previoulsy published in *Bound Together Like the Grasses* (Clover Valley Press) and is reprinted by permission of the author.

"After Thirty-Five Years," by Mara Hart, appeared in an earlier version in *Trail Guide* (Calyx Press, 2008) and is reprinted by permission of the author.

"Gooseberry Falls, Lake Superior," by Susan Carol Hauser, appeared previously under the title "Somewhere Safe to Sea" in *Beloved on the Earth: 150 Poems of Grief and Gratitude* (Holy Cow! Press, 2009) and is reprinted by permission of the author and publisher.

"I Tell the Lake a Story," by Eva Hooker, is reprinted from *Cavalier Literary Conture* (Volume 1, Number 1, 2010) by permission of the author.

"Into All Things We Enter," by Ann Iverson, was previously published in *Art Lessons* (Holy Cow! Press, 2011) and is reprinted by permission of the author and publisher.

"Spirit Little Cedar," by Susan Deborah King, was previously published in a chapbook *One Life, One Meeting* by Plymouth Congregational Church (Minneapolis, MN) and is reprinted by permission of the author.

"Easter Dawn on Superior," by Cecilia Lieder, was previously published in *Haiku Journey* (Calyx Press, 2014) and is reprinted by permission of the author.

"Shovel Point," by Judy Lindberg, was previously published in an earlier version in *Shovel Point* (Flume Press, Chico, CA) and in *The Madison Revew* and is reprinted by permission of the author.

"Key Sequences Missing," by Micky McGilligan, was exhibited with a photograph by Chris Dahlberg at Waterfront Gallery, Two Harbors, Minnesota in the "Words to Art" exhibit (2013) and is reprinted by permission of the author.

"Poet Laureate of Duluth," by Pamela Mittlefehldt, was previously published in *Trail Guide to the Northland Experience in Prints and Poetry* (Calyx Press, 2008) and is reprinted by permission of the author.

"Temperance 2020," by Susan Perala-Dewey, first appeared in *Thunderbird Review* (2013) and is reprinted by permission of the author.

"Morning," by Ellie Schoenfeld, is reprinted from *Morning— Difficult Valentines* (Fallow Deer Books, 2004); "An Unrefined Northern Metaphor," by Elle Schoenfeld, is reprinted from *Bound Together Like the Grasses* (Clover Valley Press, 2013) by permission of the author.

"Mining Country," by Steven Sher, first appeared in *Seems* (Volume 38, 2005) and in a collection by the author (*Skipping Stones,* Finishing Line Press, 2011) and is reprinted by permission of the author.

"Lake Superior—A Love Song from the Lake (lyrics)," by Sara Thomsen, is from *Winter Wanderings,* CD, 2010. All rights reserved, copyright 2010 by Sara Thomsen. Reprinted by permission of Sara Thomsen.

About the Cover Artist

Nancy Hemstad Seaton lives and works at Hungry Jack Outfitters on the Gunflint Trail outside of Grand Marais, MN. Lake Superior inspires her every time she heads down the hill to town. She earned her BA from St. Olaf College and teaches classes at the Grand Marais Art Colony. More of her work can be seen at Sivertson Gallery in Grand Marais or *www.sivertson.com*.

About the Lake Superior Artists

AJ Atwater is a Manhattan/Minnesota artist, art blogger and literary fiction writer. Contact her at *ajatwater.com*.

Sarah M. Brokke lives and works in Duluth, MN. Her work has been exhibited nationally and internationally, and she is the Director of the Art Department at the College of St. Scholastica.

Joel Cooper has been screen printing fine art prints since 1989. His work reflects living on the shores of Lake Superior in Duluth and in Cornucopia... *www.cooperartpoetry.com*.

Cecilia Lieder is a poet and original print artist working in woodcut and stone lithography. She has lived beside Lake Superior most of her life and been profoundly shaped by it. More of her works can be found at *www.cecilialieder.com*.

Alberta Marana is a landscape artist who has been reflecting the beauty of northern Minnesota and northwestern Wisconsin for over 25 years. Her art can be found in numerous collections including the Mayo Clinic, Rochester, MN, Takeda Pharmeceutical Corp, Deerfield, IL, University of Wisconsin Hospitals, Madison, and the Tweed Museum as well as numerous other public and private collections. Her website is *albertamarana.com*.

Sue Pavlatos, Duluth artist, has exhibited regionally, nationally, and internationally. She is a painter, working mainly in watercolor and acrylics. Landscape, especially the Lake Superior area, has always been a favorite subject.

Penny Perry lives in Duluth and owns Perry Framing & Stained Glass. Her artworks are inspired by the wonder and intricacies of the natural world and all its inhabitants.

Thomas Rauschenfels uses wood and linoleum blocks, pencil, ink, pen, brush, and pigment, to make art on the shores of Lake Superior. The Lake, nature, and the human figure are wonderful subjects for present and future art pieces, many of which can be seen at *thomasrauschenfels.com*.

Arna Rennan started painting plein aire after years of living in Oslo, Norway, where she received her training at the Nat'l Academy of Art. It was her way of reconnecting with her surroundings. Arna's work is included in public collections by the MN ST Arts Bd PerCent for Public Art, Norshor Bank and Essentia Health. She has also juried plein aire exhibitions in Grand Marais, Aitkin, and Port Wing, Wisconsin.

Adam Swanson's work addresses the future, fragility of the human presence, perseverance of nature and underlying threads of danger that underpin societies. After three years in New York and a few stints in Antarctica, he has called northern Minnesota home since 2009. He paints full-time, is married and is the father of two. More of his work can be seen on his website *www.adamswanson.com* or at Lizzard's and Siiviis Galleries in Duluth, MN and Sivertson Gallery in Grand Marais, MN.

Jan Hartley Wise lives and works in Washburn, Wisconsin. She explores many facets of art and is represented in several area galleries.

About the Editors

Jim Perlman founded Holy Cow! Press in 1977. He and his family have lived in Duluth, Minnesota since1988, where he co-founded the Spirit Lake Poetry series, and helped establish the Duluth poet laureate project in 2005. With co-editors Deborah Cooper, Mara Hart, and Pamela Mittlefehldt, *Beloved on the Earth: 150 Poems of Grief & Gratitud*e was published in 2009; *The Heart of All That Is: Reflections on Home* was published in 2013.

Deborah Cooper is the author of five volumes of poetry and has had her work published in numerous journals and anthologies. She facilitates poetry groups at the St. Louis County Jail and was the 2012-2014 Duluth Poet Laureate.

Mara Hart has been an editor of three periodicals and three anthologies. A former librarian and teacher, she now is a writer, mentor and editor. She lives in Duluth, Minnesota with two cats and many books.

Pamela Mittlefehldt is a poet, editor, writer, and fiddler. The focus of her work is on the power of story to transform our lives as individuals and as communities. She is currently working on a cross-genre project on food, justice, place, and spirit.